ENVIRONMENTAL QUALITY
In a Growing Economy

❧ ENVIRONMENTAL QUALITY ❧
In a Growing Economy

Essays from the Sixth RFF Forum

by

Kenneth E. Boulding, Harold J. Barnett
René Dubos, Leonard J. Duhl
Ralph Turvey, Roland N. McKean
Allen V. Kneese, M. Mason Gaffney
Gilbert F. White, David Lowenthal
Norton E. Long, Jacob H. Beuscher

Edited by Henry Jarrett

Published for

RESOURCES FOR THE FUTURE, INC.

By

THE JOHNS HOPKINS PRESS

RESOURCES FOR THE FUTURE, INC.
1755 Massachusetts Avenue, N.W.,
Washington, D.C. 20036

Resources for the Future is a non-profit
corporation for research and education in
the development, conservation, and use of
natural resources. It was established in 1952
with the co-operation of the Ford Foundation
and its activities since then have been
financed by grants from that Foundation.
Part of the work of Resources for the
Future is carried out by its resident staff,
part supported by grants to universities and
other non-profit organizations. Unless otherwise stated, interpretations and conclusions
in RFF publications are those of the
authors; the organization takes responsibility
for the selection of significant subjects for
study, the competence of researchers, and
their freedom of inquiry.

This book is based on papers given at the
1966 RFF Forum on Environmental
Quality held in Washington March 8 and 9.

Director of RFF publications, Henry Jarrett;
editor, Vera W. Dodds; *associate editor,* Nora E. Roots.

Copyright © 1966, The Johns Hopkins Press,
Baltimore, Maryland 21218
Library of Congress Catalogue Card Number 66-28505

CONTENTS

EDITOR'S INTRODUCTION

Captain Donaldson, a retired glassblower who used to keep a small boatyard on the Potomac about fifteen miles below Washington, was, at the time I knew him late in his life, deeply exasperated at the condition of the river. "When I first came here," he would say, glowering at the turbid, greenish-brown water, "you could see a corpse in ten feet." The Captain's lament of nearly twenty years ago anticipated a far wider concern that was to come later.

All over the country more and more of the pressing problems and issues of all natural resources, not just of water, are coming to be those of quality rather than quantity. This is true not only of the United States, with which this book is primarily concerned, but also of most of the other countries that have reached an advanced stage of economic development. The growth of interest in quality has led to inauguration of large-scale federal efforts to maintain or improve the natural environment, and to many efforts toward the same end by state and local governments and private groups and individuals. The goals of healthfulness and beauty are, in fact, keystones in President Johnson's concept of the Great Society.

The change in emphasis has come quickly. As recently as 1951, when President Truman established the President's Materials Policy Commission, fears of natural resource scarcity were uppermost in the minds of most people. The Commission's main assignment was to inquire into whether there would be enough food and industrial raw materials at

The twelve essays in this book were originally presented as papers at the Sixth RFF Forum, March 8 and 9, 1966. All of the papers have been revised by their authors prior to publication. Through the co-operation of Edward A. Ackerman, executive director of the Carnegie Institution, the Forum was held in the Institution's auditorium in Washington, D.C. An invited audience of about 250 attended. The Forum was planned by an RFF staff group led by Allen V. Kneese, who is director of RFF's research programs in water resources and in quality of the environment. The sessions were chaired by Joseph L. Fisher, RFF president.

reasonable prices over the next twenty-five years to support continued economic growth and meet the requirements of national security.

Today, in the middle 1960's, many of the worries over supply have subsided. For the next generation—and probably longer—there are few indications of widespread and persistent shortages of materials. Instead, the most troublesome questions are likely to concern the cleanliness of water and air; the effects of heavy use of pesticides upon soil and water; availability of suitable surroundings for outdoor recreation; the beauty of the countryside; and the effects of urban living upon the human body and spirit. These make a mixed bag of problems, but all of them can come under the tent of a single phrase: "quality of the environment."

It is of course true that the new emphasis on quality is more of a relative than an absolute change. Not all of the environmental problems were born yesterday: water pollution has been a live issue for decades, and so has air pollution in Pittsburgh, Chicago, and a few other cities; the history of national parks goes back over nearly a century, and that of some municipal parks even longer. Neither has the threat of scarcities of natural resource materials been entirely banished; even in the United States and other economically advanced countries, painful shortages of a temporary or localized nature can be expected before the end of the century. And in some of the less-developed countries many of the most urgent resource problems today remain those of scarcity.

For the more distant future everywhere, Malthus still casts a long shadow. Few economists care to make detailed projections for more than forty or fifty years, and broad opinions on prospects for the next hundred years or longer are mixed. It is interesting to note that some of the contributors to this volume, though agreed on the urgency of quality problems in the near future, are dubious of the longer-range prospects for resource adequacy; others are more hopeful. In any event, it is quite clear that if national and world populations continue to increase at anything like present rates, it is only a question of time until pressures upon both environmental quality and supplies of natural resource products become intolerable.

But even when all the important exceptions and qualifications are made, the fact remains that the recent emergence of problems of quality as a widely felt concern has created a new situation: understanding its nature and devising policies and programs to deal with its many manifestations will tax the ingenuity of the American people.

An instinctive first response to many of the signs of lowered environmental quality—smoggy atmosphere, polluted streams, noise, ugly slums, automobile graveyards, land skinned by strip mining, and so on through a long list—is to want to turn the clock back to a simpler, less crowded age. Then one realizes the futility of such a wish. The underlying causes of these discomforts and hazards are to be seen in the same statistics that most of the time are hailed as indicators of economic growth. A few outstanding examples are given below in the form of a table. More people (especially the growing majority living close together in urban areas) with more money to spend, more mobility, and more leisure, along with more production and consumption per person, result not only in a flourishing economy but also in heavier pressures on the environment—more crowding in cities and on highways, less unspoiled woodland and shoreline, more factory fumes, and more family and industrial wastes to dispose of. The welcome and the unwelcome results are two sides of the same coin. If the RFF projections from 1980 and 2000 are anywhere near the mark, the forces of economic progress working to degrade the environment will become steadily stronger.

	U.S. Population (millions)		Automobiles in use (millions)	Personal Consumption Expenditures (billions 1960 dollars)	Federal Reserve Board Index of Industrial Production (1957=100)
	Total	Urban			
1920	105.7	54.2	8.1		26.0
1940	132.1	74.4	26.2	158.9	43.6
1960	179.9	125.0	59.3	328.9	108.0
1980	245.0	193.0	120.0	662.0	249.0
2000	331.0	279.0	243.0	1,320.0	564.0

In the 1920 row the figures for automobiles in use is for 1921. The italicized figures for 1980 and 2000 are middle-range projections from *Resources in America's Future,* by Hans H. Landsberg, Leonard L. Fischman, and Joseph L. Fisher (Baltimore: The Johns Hopkins Press for Resources for the Future, 1963).

Population and economic activity have been growing in the United States for two centuries. Yet unlike worry over natural resources supply, which in many instances has developed gradually, much of the serious concern over environmental quality has arisen only recently. Many of the problems of this kind have seemed full-grown from the start; this appears to be largely a function of scale. Up to a certain level of concentration, disposal of wastes, disfigurement of the landscape, and congestion are, at worst, local irritations. Air, water, and earth-room can absorb a lot without great damage. Beyond that point real trouble ensues; differences of degree create differences of kind. Luther Gulick at the first RFF Forum in 1958 (in a paper later published in *Perspectives on Conservation,* The Johns Hopkins Press) referred to this phenomenon as "the take-off principle."

In contemplating the rural aspects of this principle, I often think of the privy on my uncle's farm in the cut-up Maryland country north of Baltimore where the coastal plain rises up to the Piedmont. This useful structure was perched on the bank of a little stream that chattered past the house and joined a larger creek about a quarter of a mile beyond. When I was a boy, the time of the First World War, this location struck me as pleasant and convenient. Some years later, after learning about sanitation, I used to wince at the memory. Still later, upon recalling that nobody in those days lived on the big creek for four or five miles downstream and the nearest neighbor on the little stream lived two miles up toward the source, I relaxed and could take pleasure in my first-hand experience of the law of concentration and take-off.

Another reason for the change in attitude is that Americans in recent years have demanded much higher levels of environmental quality. (Maybe the good old days were not really so good as they seem in retrospect.) Patient programs of education have undoubtedly accounted for part of the rise in standards, but the strongest push seems to have come from greater affluence: with something left over after buying the necessities, people can afford to take more interest in some of the higher things, whether through larger taxes or larger personal expenditures.

Resource problems of quality differ from those of quantity in several respects, at least two of which profoundly affect people's ways of coping with them.

1. The quality problems tend to be much broader and more open-ended. Most of the quantity problems, difficult though they are, have fairly sharp definitions. Within the accepted rules of the game in our modified free-enterprise economy, how does one obtain a continuing adequate supply of resource materials at relatively low real cost? (Or, in the case of U.S. farm products, how does one deal with at least a short-term surplus?) In any case, the ultimate objective is the production and distribution of rather clearly defined natural resource goods or services that people need or at least will pay for. But when one moves into the problems of environmental quality, the field is wide open. The only absolute limits are those of what is physically possible, and as technology advances it becomes harder to say where those limits lie. The basic question usually is: "What kind of environment do we want?"

How important is it to curb billboards and neon-lighted hot dog stands along the highways? How clean do we really want our air and streams to be? These and scores of other puzzling questions lie close to the surface. One can go deeper and ask whether larger production of material goods is always *ipso facto* a good thing or ask whether man's adaptability over the short term will in the longer run be a blessing or a curse.

2. The solutions to problems of quality, insofar as goals can be agreed on, lie to a large extent outside the influence of the market economy. Despite the extensive degree of government intervention or outright control in the supply and distribution of resource goods and services in the mixed economy of the United States, the free market still is the main mechanism for handling the quantitative side of resource management. Government (federal, state, or local) may impose all kinds of regulations or even go into business itself; still it is primarily through the price system that supplies are produced and allocated. But in matters of quality the market system often functions poorly or not at all. The production, distribution, and use of natural resources often have profound effects upon persons not directly concerned in these activities. Yet such side effects are rarely bought or sold. (The effects can be good as well as bad, although the unfavorable ones get most of the attention.) The most familiar example, perhaps, is dumping of wastes in rivers. The town or factory which does so is using a cheap disposal method from the standpoint of its own profit accounting but the cost to people downstream—either in the form of purifying the water or suffering unpleasant sights and smells—may be high. Other examples are air pollution from automobile exhausts or industrial fumes—cheap disposal methods for both—or the noise that neighbors suffer from the operation of an airport.

The market mechanism doesn't work very well, because in these and similar situations the controlling relationships are not between buyers and sellers. Some redress can be got through civil or criminal law, or government regulation or taxation, but the results have seldom been adequate or even-handed. There is a clear need for more study and experimentation in the field of political and social action.

Written history and archaeological evidence before that tell of a continuous effort to wrest more food and raw materials from the earth. Some say that Western man has laid too much emphasis on materials, though only recently have the great mass of people, even in the most advanced countries, enjoyed the expectation of enough food, clothing, and shelter. Now that in the United States and a few other developed countries adequate supply seems assured, at least for the near future, the scale of farm and industrial production and of transport, and the spread of urbanization are threatening other human values—the very values that more people are coming to emphasize because they can afford them.

Granting that most of the pressures upon the natural environment have been direct or indirect results of a prosperous and expanding economy, does it follow that further erosion of environmental quality must continue to be the price of further economic gains? There is no pat answer. The most one can say is that continued decline does not appear inevitable. On the hopeful side are a vigorous technology and a capacity—if pressed hard enough—for political innovation and social discipline. On the other side are the difficulty and unfamiliarity of some of the present and prospective problems. Even a tolerable degree of success will not come easily.

It is time to take soundings, as several government and private groups are doing. This was the purpose of the Resources for the Future Forum on Environmental Quality that was held in March 1966.

In view of the limitations of any one symposium—or any one book—the coverage is selective. There is almost no limit to the avenues that might be explored and the distances down each that might be traveled in an exhaustive examination of the problems of environmental quality. The effort here is to touch upon some of the highlights of the current situation, to look at the prospects, and to ask what might be done about them. Six topics were chosen. For each, one expert in his field was asked to prepare a paper and another to respond either by critical comment, development of other aspects of the problem, or both. These papers, as subsequently revised in the light of comment and discussion at the Forum, constitute the essays in this book.

In the first pair of essays, Kenneth Boulding and Harold Barnett open the inquiry with a broad look at how development of natural resources has affected the environment and may be expected to affect it in the future. Mr. Boulding, while recognizing the importance of many near-term problems, takes the long view, with a critical look at goals and values that often are taken for granted. Seeing the advance of technology and the growth of population as forces that are making it increasingly plain that the Planet Earth is a self-contained spaceship with diminishing new sources of materials and less and less room for disposal of wastes, he questions the familiar idea that continuingly increasing pro-

duction and consumption of goods are in themselves desirable. Mr.
Barnett, while limiting his horizon largely to the end of the twentieth
century, explores the effects of economic growth upon the natural environment, and asks whether the ideal of a competitive self-regulating
market will be as useful in the decades ahead as it was in the nineteenth
century and the first part of the twentieth.

The second pair of essays deals with almost as broad a subject:
effects of the environment upon human health, both physical and mental. René Dubos sees a crucial problem in the contrast between man's
biological stability—no perceptible change since our Cro-Magnon fore-
bears—and his formidable capacity to form new social and cultural
patterns and to survive, at least for many years, under new conditions.
Because of man's adaptability some apparently harmless effects of urban
living may begin to take their toll decades later and in indirect ways.
Furthermore, who can say whether man's remarkable capacity to adapt
will always carry him in what by present values appear to be desirable
directions? Leonard J. Duhl, interested mainly in mental health, sees,
along with Dr. Dubos, the spread of urbanization as the central issue.
Fragmentation, he believes, causes much of the difficulty—a tendency
to take a piecemeal approach instead of viewing the complex problem
of city living as a whole. As things stand, municipal agencies are intent
on only their particular programs and individuals are subject to conflicting pressures from many quarters. He sees need for new institutions
to put the bewildering pieces of the picture together.

The fact that many of the economic problems of environmental
quality are caused or aggravated by lying outside the market economy
raises many problems and possibilities that have not been well explored.
Ralph Turvey, noting that the market mechanism fails when economic
decisions concerning the use of natural resources do not take account
of all the effects of such use, analyzes the nature of the side effects that
slip through the slats and suggests possible ways of coping with them.
Roland McKean, going farther along a couple of the paths opened by
Mr. Turvey, examines the practical problems of establishing criteria and
acquiring the information needed in programs that can deal with the
principal side effects of resource use.

Establishment of both goals and methods will call for much more
knowledge than is now available. The fourth set of essays examines the
current state of economic research into the problems of the environment.
Allen V. Kneese discusses research goals, progress made toward them
thus far, and the major tasks that remain to be undertaken. In the
course of his critical survey he cites a number of examples of projects

now under way by public and private agencies, including Resources for the Future. Mason Gaffney, without paralleling Mr. Kneese's detailed material, explores some of the general problems of environmental research in the light of welfare economics, and supplements Mr. Kneese's findings on research gaps with further suggestions of urgently needed lines of inquiry.

What kind of environment do Americans want and how much are they willing to pay for it in money and effort? The fact that modern man has a wide range of choices which must be made without the aid of the semi-automatic functioning of the market heightens the importance of public attitudes that affect political and private action. How are such attitudes formed and how can they be measured and evaluated? These questions are considered in the fifth pair of essays. Gilbert White surveys this broad field that is in the process of changing from an art to a science, noting the progress that has been made and the large amount of work, including fundamental research, that still needs to be done. David Lowenthal steps back a few paces to consider the assumptions that lie behind public attitudes on questions of environmental quality.

Then there are the problems of taking action to maintain or improve the environment. Here public policies and social and political institutions are of great importance. Many of the nation's current policies and institutions date from times of simple technology and a smaller, more rural, population. And although man can change his social patterns profoundly he rarely does so willingly or quickly. Norton Long, in the first of the final pair of essays, reviews the new tasks that confront government at national, state, and local levels and gives special attention to the interaction among them under a federal system. Jacob Beuscher suggests some of the new kinds of governmental machinery that might be used, including joint boards and compacts for interstate action, methods of operation in metropolitan regions, and the role of state courts.

It is clear at a glance that this book leaves out more than it puts in. Several other important aspects of the environmental problem could have been included and those that are covered could have been treated from other viewpoints and in much more detail. Any reader expecting a comprehensive account of the state of the natural environment in the United States in the 1960's, of the events that brought things to their present pass, or of the dangers and opportunities that lie ahead will not find it here. What he will find is a wide-ranging collection of impres-

sions, interpretations, and reports of research findings by scholars of varying interests and experience who have given years of thought to one or
another of the salient pieces of the problem. As a collection, the essays
should contribute to a fuller understanding of what has been happening
to land, water, and air in the United States, particularly in cities and
suburbs. It should also contribute to an appreciation of how much needs
to be done to make this country a better place to live in, and a better
idea of how groups and individuals can go about doing it.

June, 1966   HENRY JARRETT
Washington, D.C.   Resources for the Future

Chapter One

RESOURCES DEVELOPMENT AND THE ENVIRONMENT

Kenneth E. Boulding

THE ECONOMICS OF THE COMING SPACESHIP EARTH

We are now in the middle of a long process of transition in the nature of the image which man has of himself and his environment. Primitive men, and to a large extent also men of the early civilizations, imagined themselves to be living on a virtually illimitable plane. There was almost always somewhere beyond the known limits of human habitation, and over a very large part of the time that man has been on earth, there has been something like a frontier. That is, there was always some place else to go when things got too difficult, either by reason of the deterioration of the natural environment or a deterioration of the social structure in places where people happened to live. The image of the frontier is probably one of the oldest images of mankind, and it is not surprising that we find it hard to get rid of.

Gradually, however, man has been accustoming himself to the notion of the spherical earth and a closed sphere of human activity. A few unusual spirits among the ancient Greeks perceived that the earth was a sphere. It was only with the circumnavigations and the geographical explorations of the fifteenth and sixteenth centuries, however, that the fact that the earth was a sphere became at all widely known and accepted. Even in the nineteenth century, the commonest map was Mercator's projection, which visualizes the earth as an illimitable cylinder, essentially a plane wrapped around the globe, and it was not until the Second World War and the development of the air age that the global

Kenneth E. Boulding *is professor of economics at the University of Michigan and author of numerous books, pamphlets, and articles. His most recent book,* The Meaning of the Twentieth Century, *was published in 1964. A fourth edition of his* Economics Analyses, *first published in 1941, came out in 1965. Mr. Boulding was born in Liverpool, England, in 1910 and received his B.A. and M.A. degrees from Oxford University. He became a United States citizen in 1948. Before going to the University of Michigan in 1949, he taught at universities in Scotland, Canada, and the United States.*

nature of the planet really entered the popular imagination. Even now we are very far from having made the moral, political, and psychological adjustments which are implied in this transition from the illimitable plane to the closed sphere.

Economists in particular, for the most part, have failed to come to grips with the ultimate consequences of the transition from the open to the closed earth. One hesitates to use the terms "open" and "closed" in this connection, as they have been used with so many different shades of meaning. Nevertheless, it is hard to find equivalents. The open system, indeed, has some similarities to the open system of von Bertalanffy,[1] in that it implies that some kind of a structure is maintained in the midst of a throughput from inputs to outputs. In a closed system, the outputs of all parts of the system are linked to the inputs of other parts. There are no inputs from outside and no outputs to the outside; indeed, there is no outside at all. Closed systems, in fact, are very rare in human experience, in fact almost by definition unknowable, for if there are genuinely closed systems around us, we have no way of getting information into them or out of them; and hence if they are really closed, we would be quite unaware of their existence. We can only find out about a closed system if we participate in it. Some isolated primitive societies may have approximated to this, but even these had to take inputs from the environment and give outputs to it. All living organisms, including man himself, are open systems. They have to receive inputs in the shape of air, food, water, and give off outputs in the form of effluvia and excrement. Deprivation of input of air, even for a few minutes, is fatal. Deprivation of the ability to obtain any input or to dispose of any output is fatal in a relatively short time. All human societies have likewise been open systems. They receive inputs from the earth, the atmosphere, and the waters, and they give outputs into these reservoirs; they also produce inputs internally in the shape of babies and outputs in the shape of corpses. Given a capacity to draw upon inputs and to get rid of outputs, an open system of this kind can persist indefinitely.

There are some systems—such as the biological phenotype, for instance the human body—which cannot maintain themselves indefinitely by inputs and outputs because of the phenomenon of aging. This process is very little understood. It occurs, evidently, because there are some outputs which cannot be replaced by any known input. There is not the same necessity for aging in organizations and in societies, although an analogous phenomenon may take place. The structure and composition

[1] Ludwig von Bertalanffy, *Problems of Life* (New York: John Wiley and Sons, 1952).

of an organization or society, however, can be maintained by inputs of fresh personnel from birth and education as the existing personnel ages and eventually dies. Here we have an interesting example of a system which seems to maintain itself by the self-generation of inputs, and in this sense is moving towards closure. The input of people (that is, babies) is also an output of people (that is, parents).

Systems may be open or closed in respect to a number of classes of inputs and outputs. Three important classes are matter, energy, and information. The present world economy is open in regard to all three. We can think of the world economy or "econosphere" as a subset of the "world set," which is the set of all objects of possible discourse in the world. We then think of the state of the econosphere at any one moment as being the total capital stock, that is, the set of all objects, people, organizations, and so on, which are interesting from the point of view of the system of exchange. This total stock of capital is clearly an open system in the sense that it has inputs and outputs, inputs being production which adds to the capital stock, outputs being consumption which subtracts from it. From a material point of view, we see objects passing from the noneconomic into the economic set in the process of production, and we similarly see products passing out of the economic set as their value becomes zero. Thus we see the econosphere as a material process involving the discovery and mining of fossil fuels, ores, etc., and at the other end a process by which the effluents of the system are passed out into noneconomic reservoirs—for instance, the atmosphere and the oceans—which are not appropriated and do not enter into the exchange system.

From the point of view of the energy system, the econosphere involves inputs of available energy in the form, say, of water power, fossil fuels, or sunlight, which are necessary in order to create the material throughput and to move matter from the noneconomic set into the economic set or even out of it again; and energy itself is given off by the system in a less available form, mostly in the form of heat. These inputs of available energy must come either from the sun (the energy supplied by other stars being assumed to be negligible) or it may come from the earth itself, either through its internal heat or through its energy of rotation or other motions, which generate, for instance, the energy of the tides. Agriculture, a few solar machines, and water power use the current available energy income. In advanced societies this is supplemented very extensively by the use of fossil fuels, which represent as it were a capital stock of stored-up sunshine. Because of this capital stock of energy, we have been able to maintain an energy input into the system, particularly over the last two centuries, much larger than we would have been able to do with existing techniques if we had had to rely on the current input of available energy from the sun or the earth itself. This supplementary input, however, is by its very nature exhaustible.

The inputs and outputs of information are more subtle and harder to trace, but also represent an open system, related to, but not wholly dependent on, the transformations of matter and energy. By far the larger amount of information and knowledge is self-generated by the human society, though a certain amount of information comes into the sociosphere in the form of light from the universe outside. The information that comes from the universe has certainly affected man's image of himself and of his environment, as we can easily visualize if we suppose that we lived on a planet with a total cloud-cover that kept out all information from the exterior universe. It is only in very recent times, of course, that the information coming in from the universe has been captured and coded into the form of a complex image of what the universe is like outside the earth; but even in primitive times, man's perception of the heavenly bodies has always profoundly affected his image of earth and of himself. It is the information generated within the planet, however, and particularly that generated by man himself, which forms by far the larger part of the information system. We can think of the stock of knowledge, or as Teilhard de Chardin called it, the "noosphere," and consider this as an open system, losing knowledge through aging and death and gaining it through birth and education and the ordinary experience of life.

From the human point of view, knowledge or information is by far the most important of the three systems. Matter only acquires significance and only enters the sociosphere or the econosphere insofar as it becomes an object of human knowledge. We can think of capital, indeed, as frozen knowledge or knowledge imposed on the material world in the form of improbable arrangements. A machine, for instance, originated in the mind of man, and both its construction and its use involve information processes imposed on the material world by man himself. The cumulation of knowledge, that is, the excess of its production over its consumption, is the key to human development of all kinds, especially to economic development. We can see this pre-eminence of knowledge very clearly in the experiences of countries where the material capital has been destroyed by a war, as in Japan and Germany. The knowledge of the people was not destroyed, and it did not take long, therefore, certainly not more than ten years, for most of the material capital to be reestablished again. In a country such as Indonesia, however, where the knowledge did not exist, the material capital did not come into being either. By "knowledge" here I mean, of course, the whole cognitive structure, which includes valuations and motivations as well as images of the factual world.

The concept of entropy, used in a somewhat loose sense, can be applied to all three of these open systems. In the case of material systems, we can distinguish between entropic processes, which take concentrated materials and diffuse them through the oceans or over the earth's surface or into the atmosphere, and anti-entropic processes, which take diffuse materials and concentrate them. Material entropy can be taken as a measure of the uniformity of the distribution of elements and, more uncertainly, compounds and other structures on the earth's surface. There is, fortunately, no law of increasing material entropy, as there is in the corresponding case of energy, as it is quite possible to concentrate diffused materials if energy inputs are allowed. Thus the processes for fixation of nitrogen from the air, processes for the extraction of magnesium or other elements from the sea, and processes for the desalinization of sea water are anti-entropic in the material sense, though the reduction of material entropy has to be paid for by inputs of energy and also inputs of information, or at least a stock of information in the system. In regard to matter, therefore, a closed system is conceivable, that is, a system in which there is neither increase nor decrease in material entropy. In such a system all outputs from consumption would constantly be recycled to become inputs for production, as for instance, nitrogen in the nitrogen cycle of the natural ecosystem.

In regard to the energy system there is, unfortunately, no escape from the grim Second Law of Thermodynamics; and if there were no energy inputs into the earth, any evolutionary or developmental process would be impossible. The large energy inputs which we have obtained from fossil fuels are strictly temporary. Even the most optimistic predictions would expect the easily available supply of fossil fuels to be exhausted in a mere matter of centuries at present rates of use. If the rest of the world were to rise to American standards of power consumption, and still more if world population continues to increase, the exhaustion of fossil fuels would be even more rapid. The development of nuclear energy has improved this picture, but has not fundamentally altered it, at least in present technologies, for fissionable material is still relatively scarce. If we should achieve the economic use of energy through fusion, of course, a much larger source of energy materials would be available, which would expand the time horizons of supplementary energy input into an open social system by perhaps tens to hundreds of thousands of years. Failing this, however, the time is not very far distant, historically speaking, when man will once more have to retreat to his current energy input from the sun, even though this could be used much more effectively than in the past with increased knowledge. Up to now, certainly, we have not got very far with the technology of using current solar energy, but the possibility of substantial improvements in the future is certainly high. It may be, indeed, that the biological revolution which is just beginning will produce a solution to this problem, as we develop artificial organisms which are capable of much more efficient transformation of solar energy into easily available forms than any that we now have. As Richard Meier has suggested, we may run our machines in the future with methane-producing algae.[2]

The question of whether there is anything corresponding to entropy in the information system is a puzzling one, though of great interest. There are certainly many examples of social systems and cultures which have lost knowledge, especially in transition from one generation to the next, and in which the culture has therefore degenerated. One only has to look at the folk culture of Appalachian migrants to American cities to see a culture which started out as a fairly rich European folk culture in Elizabethan times and which seems to have lost both skills, adaptability, folk tales, songs, and almost everything that goes up to make richness and complexity in a culture, in the course of about ten generations. The American Indians on reservations provide another example of such degradation of the information and knowledge system. On the other hand, over a great part of human history, the growth of knowledge in the earth as a whole seems to have been almost continuous, even though there have been times of relatively slow growth and times of rapid growth. As it is knowledge of certain kinds that produces the growth of knowledge in general, we have here a very subtle and complicated system, and it is hard to put one's finger on the particular elements in a culture which make knowledge grow more or less rapidly, or even which make it decline. One of the great puzzles in this connection, for instance, is why the take-off into science, which represents an "acceleration," or an increase in the rate of growth of knowledge in European society in the sixteenth century, did not take place in China, which at that time (about 1600) was unquestionably ahead of Europe, and one would think even more ready for the breakthrough. This is perhaps the most crucial question in the theory of social development, yet we must confess that it is very little understood. Perhaps the most significant factor in this connection is the existence of "slack" in the culture, which permits a divergence from established patterns and activity which is not merely

---

[2] Richard L. Meier, *Science and Economic Development* (New York: John Wiley and Sons, 1956).

devoted to reproducing the existing society but is devoted to changing it. China was perhaps too well-organized and had too little slack in its society to produce the kind of acceleration which we find in the somewhat poorer and less well-organized but more diverse societies of Europe.

The closed earth of the future requires economic principles which are somewhat different from those of the open earth of the past. For the sake of picturesqueness, I am tempted to call the open economy the "cowboy economy," the cowboy being symbolic of the illimitable plains and also associated with reckless, exploitative, romantic, and violent behavior, which is characteristic of open societies. The closed economy of the future might similarly be called the "spaceman" economy, in which the earth has become a single spaceship, without unlimited reservoirs of anything, either for extraction or for pollution, and in which, therefore, man must find his place in a cyclical ecological system which is capable of continuous reproduction of material form even though it cannot escape having inputs of energy. The difference between the two types of economy becomes most apparent in the attitude towards consumption. In the cowboy economy, consumption is regarded as a good thing and production likewise; and the success of the economy is measured by the amount of the throughput from the "factors of production," a part of which, at any rate, is extracted from the reservoirs of raw materials and noneconomic objects, and another part of which is output into the reservoirs of pollution. If there are infinite reservoirs from which material can be obtained and into which effluvia can be deposited, then the throughput is at least a plausible measure of the success of the economy. The gross national product is a rough measure of this total throughput. It should be possible, however, to distinguish that part of the GNP which is derived from exhaustible and that which is derived from reproducible resources, as well as that part of consumption which represents effluvia and that which represents input into the productive system again. Nobody, as far as I know, has ever attempted to break down the GNP in this way, although it would be an interesting and extremely important exercise, which is unfortunately beyond the scope of this paper.

By contrast, in the spaceman economy, throughput is by no means a desideratum, and is indeed to be regarded as something to be minimized rather than maximized. The essential measure of the success of the economy is not production and consumption at all, but the nature, extent, quality, and complexity of the total capital stock, including in this the state of the human bodies and minds included in the system. In the spaceman economy, what we are primarily concerned with is stock

maintenance, and any technological change which results in the maintenance of a given total stock with a lessened throughput (that is, less
production and consumption) is clearly a gain. This idea that both
production and consumption are bad things rather than good things is
very strange to economists, who have been obsessed with the income-
flow concepts to the exclusion, almost, of capital-stock concepts.

There are actually some very tricky and unsolved problems involved
in the questions as to whether human welfare or well-being is to be
regarded as a stock or a flow. Something of both these elements seems
actually to be involved in it, and as far as I know there have been
practically no studies directed towards identifying these two dimensions
of human satisfaction. Is it, for instance, eating that is a good thing, or
is it being well fed? Does economic welfare involve having nice clothes,
fine houses, good equipment, and so on, or is it to be measured by the
depreciation and the wearing out of these things? I am inclined myself
to regard the stock concept as most fundamental, that is, to think of
being well fed as more important than eating, and to think even of
so-called services as essentially involving the restoration of a depleting
psychic capital. Thus I have argued that we go to a concert in order
to restore a psychic condition which might be called "just having gone
to a concert," which, once established, tends to depreciate. When it
depreciates beyond a certain point, we go to another concert in order
to restore it. If it depreciates rapidly, we go to a lot of concerts; if it
depreciates slowly, we go to few. On this view, similarly, we eat primarily to restore bodily homeostasis, that is, to maintain a condition
of being well fed, and so on. On this view, there is nothing desirable in
consumption at all. The less consumption we can maintain a given state
with, the better off we are. If we had clothes that did not wear out,
houses that did not depreciate, and even if we could maintain our bodily
condition without eating, we would clearly be much better off.

It is this last consideration, perhaps, which makes one pause. Would
we, for instance, really want an operation that would enable us to restore
all our bodily tissues by intravenous feeding while we slept? Is there
not, that is to say, a certain virtue in throughput itself, in activity itself,
in production and consumption itself, in raising food and in eating it?
It would certainly be rash to exclude this possibility. Further interesting
problems are raised by the demand for variety. We certainly do not
want a constant state to be maintained; we want fluctuations in the
state. Otherwise there would be no demand for variety in food, for
variety in scene, as in travel, for variety in social contact, and so on.
The demand for variety can, of course, be costly, and sometimes it
seems to be too costly to be tolerated or at least legitimated, as in the

case of marital partners, where the maintenance of a homeostatic state in the family is usually regarded as much more desirable than the variety and excessive throughput of the libertine. There are problems here which the economics profession has neglected with astonishing singlemindedness. My own attempts to call attention to some of them, for instance, in two articles,[3] as far as I can judge, produced no response whatever; and economists continue to think and act as if production, consumption, throughput, and the GNP were the sufficient and adequate measure of economic success.

It may be said, of course, why worry about all this when the spaceman economy is still a good way off (at least beyond the lifetimes of any now living), so let us eat, drink, spend, extract and pollute, and be as merry as we can, and let posterity worry about the spaceship earth. It is always a little hard to find a convincing answer to the man who says, "What has posterity ever done for me?" and the conservationist has always had to fall back on rather vague ethical principles postulating identity of the individual with some human community or society which extends not only back into the past but forward into the future. Unless the individual identifies with some community of this kind, conservation is obviously "irrational." Why should we not maximize the welfare of this generation at the cost of posterity? *"Après nous, le déluge"* has been the motto of not insignificant numbers of human societies. The only answer to this, as far as I can see, is to point out that the welfare of the individual depends on the extent to which he can identify himself with others, and that the most satisfactory individual identity is that which identifies not only with a community in space but also with a community extending over time from the past into the future. If this kind of identity is recognized as desirable, then posterity has a voice, even if it does not have a vote; and in a sense, if its voice can influence votes, it has votes too. This whole problem is linked up with the much larger one of the determinants of the morale, legitimacy, and "nerve" of a society, and there is a great deal of historical evidence to suggest that a society which loses its identity with posterity and which loses its positive image of the future loses also its capacity to deal with present problems, and soon falls apart.[4]

Even if we concede that posterity is relevant to our present problems, we still face the question of time-discounting and the closely related

[3] K. E. Boulding, "The Consumption Concept in Economic Theory," *American Economic Review*, 35:2 (May 1945), pp. 1–14; and "Income or Welfare?," *Review of Economic Studies*, 17 (1949–50), pp. 77–86.
[4] Fred L. Polak, *The Image of the Future*, Vols. I and II, translated by Elise Boulding (New York: Sythoff, Leyden and Oceana, 1961).

question of uncertainty-discounting. It is a well-known phenomenon that individuals discount the future, even in their own lives. The very existence of a positive rate of interest may be taken as at least strong supporting evidence of this hypothesis. If we discount our own future, it is certainly not unreasonable to discount posterity's future even more, even if we do give posterity a vote. If we discount this at 5 per cent per annum, posterity's vote or dollar halves every fourteen years as we look into the future, and after even a mere hundred years it is pretty small—only about 1½ cents on the dollar. If we add another 5 per cent for uncertainty, even the vote of our grandchildren reduces almost to insignificance. We can argue, of course, that the ethical thing to do is not to discount the future at all, that time-discounting is mainly the result of myopia and perspective, and hence is an illusion which the moral man should not tolerate. It is a very popular illusion, however, and one that must certainly be taken into consideration in the formulation of policies. It explains, perhaps, why conservationist policies almost have to be sold under some other excuse which seems more urgent, and why, indeed, necessities which are visualized as urgent, such as defense, always seem to hold priority over those which involve the future.

All these considerations add some credence to the point of view which says that we should not worry about the spaceman economy at all, and that we should just go on increasing the GNP and indeed the gross world product, or GWP, in the expectation that the problems of the future can be left to the future, that when scarcities arise, whether this is of raw materials or of pollutable reservoirs, the needs of the then present will determine the solutions of the then present, and there is no use giving ourselves ulcers by worrying about problems that we really do not have to solve. There is even high ethical authority for this point of view in the New Testament, which advocates that we should take no thought for tomorrow and let the dead bury their dead. There has always been something rather refreshing in the view that we should live like the birds, and perhaps posterity is for the birds in more senses than one; so perhaps we should all call it a day and go out and pollute something cheerfully. As an old taker of thought for the morrow, however, I cannot quite accept this solution; and I would argue, furthermore, that tomorrow is not only very close, but in many respects it is already here. The shadow of the future spaceship, indeed, is already falling over our spendthrift merriment. Oddly enough, it seems to be in pollution rather than in exhaustion that the problem is first becoming salient. Los Angeles has run out of air, Lake Erie has become a cesspool, the oceans are getting full of lead and DDT, and the atmosphere may become man's major problem in another generation, at the rate at which we are filling it up with gunk. It is, of course, true that at least on a microscale, things have been worse at times in the past. The cities of today, with all their foul air and polluted waterways, are probably not as bad as the filthy cities of the pretechnical age. Nevertheless, that fouling of the nest which has been typical of man's activity in the past on a local scale now seems to be extending to the whole world society; and one certainly cannot view with equanimity the present rate of pollution of any of the natural reservoirs, whether the atmosphere, the lakes, or even the oceans.

I would argue strongly also that our obsession with production and consumption to the exclusion of the "state" aspects of human welfare distorts the process of technological change in a most undesirable way. We are all familiar, of course, with the wastes involved in planned obsolescence, in competitive advertising, and in poor quality of consumer goods. These problems may not be so important as the "view with alarm" school indicates, and indeed the evidence at many points is conflicting. New materials especially seem to edge towards the side of improved durability, such as, for instance, neolite soles for footwear, nylon socks, wash and wear shirts, and so on. The case of household equipment and automobiles is a little less clear. Housing and building construction generally almost certainly has declined in durability since the Middle Ages, but this decline also reflects a change in tastes towards flexibility and fashion and a need for novelty, so that it is not easy to assess. What is clear is that no serious attempt has been made to assess the impact over the whole of economic life of changes in durability, that is, in the ratio of capital in the widest possible sense to income. I suspect that we have underestimated, even in our spendthrift society, the gains from increased durability, and that this might very well be one of the places where the price system needs correction through government-sponsored research and development. The problems which the spaceship earth is going to present, therefore, are not all in the future by any means, and a strong case can be made for paying much more attention to them in the present than we now do.

It may be complained that the considerations I have been putting forth relate only to the very long run, and they do not much concern our immediate problems. There may be some justice in this criticism, and my main excuse is that other writers have dealt adequately with the more immediate problems of deterioration in the quality of the environment. It is true, for instance, that many of the immediate problems of pollution of the atmosphere or of bodies of water arise because of the failure of the price system, and many of them could be solved by corrective taxation. If people had to pay the losses due to the nuisances which they create, a good deal more resources would go into the prevention of nuisances. These arguments involving external economies and diseconomies are familiar to economists, and there is no need to recapitulate them. The law of torts is quite inadequate to provide for the correction of the price system which is required, simply because where damages are widespread and their incidence on any particular person is small, the ordinary remedies of the civil law are quite inadequate and inappropriate. There needs, therefore, to be special legislation to cover these cases, and though such legislation seems hard to get in practice, mainly because of the widespread and small personal incidence of the injuries, the technical problems involved are not insuperable. If we were to adopt in principle a law for tax penalties for social damages, with an apparatus for making assessments under it, a very large proportion of current pollution and deterioration of the environment would be prevented. There are tricky problems of equity involved, particularly where old established nuisances create a kind of "right by purchase" to perpetuate themselves, but these are problems again which a few rather arbitrary decisions can bring to some kind of solution.

The problems which I have been raising in this paper are of larger scale and perhaps much harder to solve than the more practical and immediate problems of the above paragraph. Our success in dealing with the larger problems, however, is not unrelated to the development of skill in the solution of the more immediate and perhaps less difficult problems. One can hope, therefore, that as a succession of mounting crises, especially in pollution, arouse public opinion and mobilize support for the solution of the immediate problems, a learning process will be set in motion which will eventually lead to an appreciation of and perhaps solutions for the larger ones. My neglect of the immediate problems, therefore, is in no way intended to deny their importance, for unless we at least make a beginning on a process for solving the immediate problems we will not have much chance of solving the larger ones. On the other hand, it may also be true that a long-run vision, as it were, of the deep crisis which faces mankind may predispose people to taking more interest in the immediate problems and to devote more effort for their solution. This may sound like a rather modest optimism, but perhaps a modest optimism is better than no optimism at all.

Harold J. Barnett

❧ PRESSURES OF GROWTH ❧
UPON ENVIRONMENT

Kenneth Boulding is a social philosopher as well as an economist. It is a pleasure to yield to his imagination, range and spirit, to ride with him on his magic carpet. But this does not make it any easier to discuss his paper. Am I to try to embellish his insights, or to paraphrase his lucid text? Does he need me to tell him that he takes great tangential sweeps around an assigned topic? Or that he showers sparks on related questions?

I will start by characterizing a system like his econosphere, which might be called the ecology of human society. By this I mean human beings and their organizations in interaction with their local, national, and world environments. I shall focus on only one aspect of this human ecology system. What happens when the size of the system increases in population and economic activity, as it has during the past hundred years and will during the next hundred?

Not merely the size, but also the character or the nature of the human ecology system will change very greatly. As Professor Boulding pointed out some years ago, agility of insects is related to small size; a mere scale enlargement of an ant or grasshopper to elephant size would be a creature not merely less agile, but structurally fragile and immobile. In like manner, a small packet for fission material emits neutrons, whereas a larger packet explodes. A river subjected to small volumes

Harold J. Barnett *is professor of economics at Washington University, St. Louis. He previously was professor of economics at Wayne State University and for four years before that, from 1955 to 1959, was on the staff of Resources for the Future as director of studies in resources and national growth. Earlier he had been an economist on the staffs of the RAND Corporation and the U.S. Bureau of Mines. He is the author of* Energy Uses and Supplies *and (with Chandler Morse) of* Scarcity and Growth, *and of numerous articles and pamphlets. Mr. Barnett was born in 1917 in Patterson, N.J. He received a B.S. degree from the University of Arkansas, an M.S. from the University of California (Berkeley), and his Ph.D. from Harvard University.*

of sewage or inputs of heat cleans and cools itself and maintains a fish population, whereas one with larger inputs loses its fish, grows algae and becomes a sewer. A New York metropolitan area is not merely 100 Kalamazoos. By analogy, then, when we notice a great increase in the size of the human ecology system, we should be ready also to observe differences—perhaps vast ones—in nature and character.

Compare the human ecology system in the United States at the close of the Civil War with that of today. The population is five times as great. Economic size, as measured by GNP, is perhaps twenty times as large. Time required to travel between New York and California has shrunk a hundredfold. In the human ecology system population and activity are growing bigger and space-time size growing smaller.

The combination of these rates of change—the growth and the shrinkage—yields a very high figure of congestion. There appears to be an explosion in what may be viewed as a rough index of congestion in the human ecology system. Nor is this all. The form of much of the growth is "unnatural." There is environmental damage from non-degradable synthetics; pesticides and other chemicals; industrial smoke, heat and waste; sonic booms and transport dangers; radioactive contaminations; billboards and junk yards. And much more radical things are apparently to come: for example, in climate control to change man's seasons; in ice-cap melting which would change his continents; and if he does not avoid major war, in gene damage and mutations which would change his being.

I think that if beings from another world were viewing the human ecology system with curiosity as our children look at a bee colony or anthill, they would observe exponential increases in environmental congestion and damage. Even with our lack of perspective because we are the inhabitants and participants, at times we sense strongly that, with our increased mastery of nature's laws, we verge on losing control of the human ecology system.

Further, precisely during the periods in which these tendencies have been observed, there has been a growth in perception of and discomfort from environmental congestion and damage. The whole populace—particularly its better-educated, wealthier, and perhaps more sensitive members—appears to want better quality in its environment. The society wants fewer slums, less land disfigurement, more open space and recreation areas, less ugliness, cleaner air and streams, and so on. For the present purposes, it is immaterial how much the increased perception and desire for environmental quality expresses psychological need for relief from increased tension of modern life and how much simply derives from increased income.

The increased pace of ecological change and the lesser willingness to bear it are two of the reasons for the growing public concern. Another reason is the uncertainty over whether the laissez faire or self-regulating market economy can satisfactorily handle the problems of environmental management. And it is this latter question that I want to discuss next.

The competitive, self-regulating market economy is one of the fairest devices ever conceived by man. But it was conceived by man and not ordained by God or nature. While we may marvel at its performance over the past century and a half, we may also question the present validity and vitality of some of its elements. The complete subjugation of land to the impersonal force of the market place—its subordination, that is, to free market exchange and use—was a conception of both heroic and grotesque proportions.

It was heroic because immediate economic welfare and progress was served magnificently in that land could be sold, mortgaged, foreclosed, built upon, planted, disfigured, irrigated, reclaimed, and disembowelled.

It was grotesque because, as Polanyi has written,

What we call land is an element of nature, inextricably interwoven with man's institutions. . . . Traditionally, land and labor are not separated, labor forms part of life, land remains part of nature, life and nature form an articulate whole. Land is thus tied up with the organization of kinship, neighborhood, craft, and creed—with tribe and temple, village, guild, and church. . . . The economic function is but one of the many vital functions of land. It invests man's life with stability; it is the site of his habitation; it is a condition of his physical safety; it is the landscape and the seasons.[1]

As I read the economic history of Western society, it may indeed have been necessary during the eighteenth and nineteenth centuries that land be torn from former uses, that tenants and small landowners be evicted, that fee simple title permit unrestrained exhaustion of forest fertility and minerals, all in order to destroy existing society and to liberate nascent industrialism, urbanism, and economic growth, into what we know as modern society.

But it is not self-evident that unrestrained private ownership and use of land is still necessary in the now well-established industrial and urban society. Once we admit that land has a special role in society and that fee simple title in land is not now essential for the maintenance of a free enterprise system, then it is proper to contemplate very major revisions in the laws and rules which govern land ownership, exchange,

---

[1] Karl Polanyi, *The Great Transformation: The Political and Economic Origins of Our Time* (Boston: Beacon Press, 1957), p. 178; originally published 1944 (New York: Rinehart and Company).

lease, and use, subject, of course, to due process. Such revisions could extend to taxation of the full amount of economic rents and their use for land preservation. They could well permit governmental purchase and ownership of all land, with private leasehold use under restrictive conditions.

Lest you think I should be credited here with very original thinking, I must point out the classical, neoclassical, and modern economists have always viewed rents as "unearned increment," which may be subjected to taxation without distortion or damage to the efficient working of the competitive self-regulating market economy. In uninterrupted line since at least the time of John Stuart Mill, who was head of the Land Reform Society which had this objective, we have been teaching this notion to our children in their elementary economics course.

The fame of Henry George—more than 2 million copies of his *Progress and Poverty* reportedly have been sold, and his single-tax doctrine is still taught in the Henry George Schools in most major cities—rests upon the notion of governmental intervention in land use and net revenues. The Conservation Movement of 1890–1920 strongly rejected laissez faire with respect to land, flatly disbelieved that private owners should have the privilege of disfiguring land, cutting timber beyond sustained yield, flooding, overcropping, undermaintaining, or permitting erosion. Finally it is not accidental that many of the examples of external economies or diseconomies which occur to us relate to environmental effects.[2] As Polanyi said, they relate to the site of our habitation, the landscape, and the seasons.

In summary, I should like to emphasize that in the economic theory of a free enterprise society, there is no necessary reason why due process appropriation of economic rent or land titles should interfere with classical economic efficiency nor why democratic decisions to place boundaries and rules on land use might not improve economic welfare.

Let us assume that the environmental problem is explosive, that we can't stand it, and that our belief in free enterprise does not require that we should. We shall then need criteria for public and governmental behavior. How much intervention should occur, what forms should it take, what magnitude of costs is permitted, how and by whom, for which types of environmental damage, how should results be measured and performance appraised, and so on?

Let me comment briefly on just two of these questions. One concerns

[2] Cf. Edward S. Mason, "The Political Economy of Resource Use," in Henry Jarrett (ed.), *Perspectives on Conservation* (Baltimore: The Johns Hopkins Press for Resources for the Future, 1958); and Tibor Scitovsky, "Two Concepts of External Economies," *Journal of Political Economy,* April 1954.

benefit-cost measurement and analysis, and the other a development in public administration that may lighten the measurement problem.

Now, my interest in benefit-cost measurement and analysis for rational decision making is, to use W. S. Gilbert's words from *The Pirates of Penzance,* "just as great as any honest man's." It is well, however, to keep in mind some facts, well-known to anyone experienced in quantitive projections. Poor measurement and analysis unfailingly contribute to erroneous conclusions, but high-quality measurement and analysis are extraordinarily difficult to come by. They are costly in effort, dollars, and time.

Also, our skill in estimating future benefits and costs in a changing world is not large, and our practice of using money market rates for discounting future streams of uncertain benefits and costs may not be fully appropriate for questions concerning social regulations of environmental quality in a perpetual society.

A third obstacle is that economic theory usually measures benefits by summing up individual preferences as expressed in market purchases at going prices and it measures costs in the same way. I doubt that this is how one should decide whether the Potomac should be made fit for recreation, or whether air pollution devices should be on all cars, or whether we should put up with sonic booms, or what to do about radio-activity and gene mutation. I suspect that our skill in measuring costs is greater than in measuring some of the benefits of changes toward higher quality environment because cost measurement indicates the volume of wages, interest, and so on, or the volume of other goods we forego, whereas the measurement of benefits frequently involves collective use of new and uncertain goods in a new and uncertain setting. The term "benefits" conveys only a very general notion of desirable things, which has to be carefully defined anew for each case, once we depart from current competitive market values. We must of course try, but at present I have somewhat more faith in measures of cost than in measures of benefit.

But my concern with the difficulties of benefit-cost measurement may be alleviated by an innovation in public administration. This is the maturation of the enormously successful consensus doctrine of the Johnson Administration into a new device for which for lack of a name I will call the Omnibus. This is the conception whereby an Administration which knows what it wants in, say, improving the quality of the environment, devises a package composed of 50 (or 100 or 1000) individual and local improvement components. Such a proposal will be supported by each voting group that would be benefited by a component and not opposed by the whole set of groups, unless their hostility to the other components outweighs support of the ones to which they are favorable.

This may sound like old-fashioned log-rolling, which usually related to natural resource projects, too. But Omnibus is really a major advance on that device. First, log-rolling was a legislative contrivance, characterized by informality, explicit and crass trading, transparent self-interest, and usually carried on in opposition to Administration leadership. The present device, which in its most comprehensive form is the Great Society, aims at improving the quality of life. It reflects a Presidential vision and dream and, therefore, needs neither cost nor benefits, but only strong leadership. It was not devised, in the first instance, to benefit localities, although these benefits, too, will be obviously forthcoming. And it rides the swell of unprecedented national prosperity for a nation now accustomed to large federal budgets, to massive federal government intervention in the nation's affairs, and to such transcendental efforts as spending $50 billion for travel to the moon.

We are on the threshold, I suggest, of Presidential and Administration decision to make very large expenditures to improve the quality of the environment. It is my guess that economic analysis will play only a minor, although perhaps significant, role in that basic decision. But it may play a major and crucial role in determining the composition of the expenditures.

Chapter Two

❧⟦ENVIRONMENT AND HUMAN HEALTH⟧☙

René Dubos

PROMISES AND HAZARDS OF MAN'S ADAPTABILITY

Pessimists lament the fact that the modern environment and ways of life are so "unnatural" that man is bound to degenerate eventually, both in body and in mind. It is true indeed that conditions in urbanized and industrialized societies are very different from those under which man evolved, and therefore make on him a variety of adaptive demands that are often stressful. Most of the diseases characteristic of modern life are the expressions of man's failures to adapt successfully to new stresses for which he had not been prepared during evolutionary development.

In reality, however, man has always lived under "unnatural" conditions. He abandoned the ways of nature by the very fact that he became human. Ever since the late Paleolithic and especially Neolithic times, he has been living physically, mentally, and socially a kind of existence that has changed, and still is changing, much too fast to permit his adjustment through biological evolution.

In animals, adaptation to environmental changes occurs chiefly through genetic changes; the genetic equipment is progressively transformed through mutation and Darwinian selection. Man in contrast now remains fundamentally the same in genetic structure even though he endlessly changes his environment. Adaptation for him occurs through a few nongenetic physiological mechanisms and especially through sociocultural processes. The genetic equipment of Cro-Magnon man has

René Dubos, *microbiologist and experimental pathologist, is a professor of The Rockefeller University in New York City. As a student of the ecology of disease, he is also deeply concerned with the effects of environment upon human life. Among his many books are* The Mirage of Health, *1959;* The Unseen World, *for which he received the Phi Beta Kappa Award in 1963; and* Man Adapting, *published in 1965. Dr. Dubos was born in Saint Brice, France, in 1901. He came to the United States in 1924 and became a citizen in 1938. He studied at the Collège Chaptal and the Institut National Agronomique in Paris and received his Ph.D. from Rutgers University in 1927.*

survived unaltered despite profound changes in the ways of life brought about by climatic and geological factors, the introduction of agriculture, and the development of urban and industrial societies. One of the extraordinary attributes of man has been his ability to adjust socially and technologically to a wide range of new environments and to new stresses without benefit of genetic evolution.

The experience of our own period suggests that man's adaptability has remained as effective as it was during the ancient past. Modern man, like his ancestors, can achieve some form of physiological and sociocultural adjustment to a very wide range of conditions, even when these appear almost incompatible with organic survival. The rapid increase in population during the nineteenth century occurred even though the proletariat was then living under conditions that most of us would find almost unbearable. In our own times human beings have managed to function in concentration camps and to survive the frightful ordeal of combat during the war!

Today, as in the past, man can adapt to environmental pollution; to intense crowding; to deficient or excessively abundant diets; to monotonous, ugly, and depressing environments. All over the world the most polluted, crowded, and traumatic cities are also the ones which have the greatest appeal and where population is increasing most rapidly. Furthermore, conditions that appear undesirable biologically need not be a handicap for economic growth. Economic wealth is produced chiefly by men and women working under high nervous tension in atmospheres contaminated with chemical fumes and in crowded offices polluted with tobacco smoke.

Because human beings are so likely to become adapted to many undesirable conditions, and because they tend at present to make economic growth the most important criterion of social betterment, it will not be easy to create a climate of opinion favorable to the immense effort needed for the control of environmental threats. Yet it is certain that many environmental factors exert a deleterious influence on important aspects of human life. As we shall now see, the reason this danger is largely overlooked is that the damage caused to human life by environmental insults is usually so delayed and indirect that it escapes recognition through the usual analysis of cause-effect relationships.

Adaptability is almost by definition an asset for survival. Yet the very fact that man possesses great ability to achieve some form of biological or social adjustment to many different forms of stress is paradoxically a source of danger for his welfare and his future. The danger comes from the fact that it is often difficult to relate the delayed and indirect pathological consequences of environmental damage to their primary cause.

Atmospheric pollution in the industrial areas of Northern Europe provides striking examples of man's ability to function in a biologically undesirable environment, as well as of the dangers inherent in this adaptability.

Ever since the beginning of the Industrial Revolution, the inhabitants of Northern Europe have been heavily exposed to many types of air pollutants produced by incomplete combustion of coal and released in the fumes from chemical plants; such exposure is rendered even more objectionable by the inclemency of the Atlantic climate. However, long experience with pollution and with bad weather has resulted in physiological reactions and living habits that have adaptive value. This is proved by the fact that Northern Europeans accept almost cheerfully their dismal atmospheric environment even though it appears almost unbearable to outsiders who experience it for the first time.

Adaptive responses to environmental pollution are not peculiar to Northern Europeans. They occur all over the world in the heavily industrialized areas whose inhabitants function effectively despite the almost constant presence of irritating substances in the air they breathe. It would seem therefore that human beings can readily make an adequate adjustment to massive air pollution.

Unfortunately, acceptance of air pollution results eventually in various forms of physiological suffering and economic loss. Even among persons who seem almost unaware of the smogs surrounding them, the respiratory tract continuously registers the insult of the various air pollutants. After periods of time that differ from one case to another, the cumulative effects of irritation commonly generate chronic bronchitis and other forms of pulmonary disease. Because this does not happen until several years later after initial exposure, it is difficult to relate the manifestations of the pathological condition to the primary physiological cause.

Chronic pulmonary disease now constitutes the greatest single medical problem in Northern Europe, as well as the most costly; it is increasing in prevalence at an alarming rate also in North America, and it will probably spread to all areas undergoing industrialization. There is good evidence, furthermore, that air pollution increases the incidence of various types of cancer as well as the numbers of fatalities among persons suffering from vascular diseases. But here again, the long and indefinite span of time between cause and effect makes it difficult to establish convincingly the etiological relationships.

The delayed effects of air pollutants constitute models for the kind of medical problems likely to arise in the future from other forms of environmental pollution. Allowing for differences in detail, the course of events can be predicted in its general trends.

Wherever socially and economically convenient, chemical pollution of air, water, and food will be sufficiently controlled to prevent the kind of toxic effects that are immediately disabling and otherwise obvious. Human beings will then tolerate without complaints concentrations of environmental pollutants (whatever their nature and origin) that they do not regard as a serious nuisance and that do not interrupt social and economic life. But it is probable that continued exposure to low levels of toxic agents will eventually result in a great variety of delayed pathological manifestations, creating much physiological misery and increasing the medical load. The point of importance here is that the worst pathological effects of environmental pollutants will not be detected at the time of exposure; indeed they may not become evident until several decades later. In other words, society will become adjusted to levels of pollution sufficiently low not to have an immediate nuisance value, but this apparent adaptation will eventually cause much pathological damage in the adult population and create large medical and social burdens.

It is well known, for example, that highly effective techniques have been developed to control the acute diseases that used to be caused by water pollution. Microbial pathogens can be held in check by chlorination; organic matter content can be minimized by dilution, oxygenation, and other chemical techniques; and of course water can be made limpid by filtration. But there is no practical technique for removing inorganic materials, as well as some synthetic organic substances, that tend to accumulate in water supplies as a result of industrial and domestic operations. Even though clear and free of pathogens, many sources of potable water are now becoming increasingly contaminated with a variety of substances that probably exert delayed toxic effects. In this regard, it is worth keeping in mind the recent reports suggesting that the incidence of certain forms of cancer and vascular diseases is correlated with differences in geological formation and in the mineral content of water supplies. While these reports are still preliminary and *sub judice,* they point to a new kind of threat to health, which, though ill-defined, bids fair to become of increasing importance in the future.

Recent physiological and behavioral studies have revealed that adjustment to the various forms of malnutrition may also have distant consequences of far-reaching importance.

Persons who have been born and raised in an environment where food intake is quantitatively or qualitatively inadequate seem to achieve a physiological adaptation to the kind of malnutrition that they have experienced in youth. Adaptation to low food intake has obvious merits for survival under conditions of scarcity but, as is now realized, it creates a vicious circle of metabolic difficulties and mental retardation or indolence. Similarly, adaptation to a very high nutritional intake probably has unfavorable consequences in the long run. Children fed diets that are excessively abundant and rich tend to become large eaters as adults —an unhealthy habit since overnutrition is associated with an increased incidence of vascular diseases.

A last example will suffice to illustrate the wide range of disease problems that can arise from adjustment to objectionable biological conditions. Immense strides have been made toward the control of the acute infectious diseases that used to be responsible for so many deaths in the past. Despite this progress, however, other kinds of microbial disease are still responsible today for a very large percentage of absenteeism from school, office, and factory. These diseases are caused by microbes that are constantly present in us or around us, but become active only when the general resistance of the body is lowered. As a result of the erroneous belief that microbial diseases have been "conquered" there is a tendency to accept the sacrifice of many days every year to so-called "minor" infections. Yet these ailments have a long-range importance far greater than their nuisance value. They erode the functional integrity of the body, progressively damaging the respiratory, digestive, and urinary tracts, as well as the kidneys and perhaps also the blood vessels. Like other stresses to which man becomes adjusted, minor infectious processes probably play an important role in the diseases of the modern world.

In view of the increase in the world population, the problems posed by adaptation to crowding bid fair to change in character and to become of increasing importance in the near future. Man is a gregarious animal; he generally tends to accept crowded environments and even to seek them. This attitude unquestionably has social advantages but these may have pathological counterparts if acceptance of crowding is carried too far. Physiological tests have revealed, for example, that crowding results in an increased secretion of various hormones; the greater activity of the adrenal cortex is of particular importance in this regard because it affects the whole human physiology. An adequate secretion of adrenal hormones is essential for well-being but an excessive secretion has a variety of deleterious effects.

Furthermore, experimental studies with various animal species have revealed that excessive crowding results in many forms of behavioral disturbances, ranging from sexual aberrations to cannibalism or—more interestingly—to complete social unresponsiveness.

Admittedly, the devastating outbreaks of disease among the nineteenth century proletariat during the Industrial Revolution were due in large part to malnutrition and unsanitary conditions. It is safe to assume, however, that the intense crowding in the tenements and factories of the mushrooming cities also was responsible for many other types of biological disturbances. These were aggravated by the fact that most members of the new labor classes had immigrated from rural areas and were totally unadapted to urban and industrial life.

The world is now becoming more and more urbanized and industrialized. Constant and intimate contact with hordes of human beings has come to constitute the "normal" way of life, and men have eagerly adjusted to it. This change has certainly brought about all kinds of phenotypic adaptations to social environments that constituted biological and emotional threats in the past.

Crowding is a relative term. Its biological significance must be evaluated in the light of the past experience of the group concerned, because this experience conditions the manner in which each of its members responds to the others as well as to environmental stimuli and trauma. Crowding *per se,* i.e., population density, is probably less important in the long run than is the intensity of social conflicts that it brings about—conflicts which become less intense after social adjustments have been made. But it is impossible at present to formulate clear policies in this regard, because so little is known concerning the density of population or the kind of stimulation best suited in the long run for the mind and the body of man.

Observations on territoriality and dominance in animal populations have thrown useful light on the physiological and behavioral effects that are likely to result from excessive crowding in human societies. In brief, there is much reason to believe that laying claim to a territory and maintaining a certain distance from one's fellow constitute biological needs that are probably as essential for man as they are for animals. However, the expressions of these needs are culturally conditioned. The distance considered proper between persons in a group varies from culture to culture. People reared in cultures where close contacts are good manners appear "pushy" to those belonging to social groups in which propriety demands greater physical separation. In contrast, the latter will appear to the former as behaving in a cold, aloof, withdrawn, and standoffish manner.

Although social anthropologists have not yet adequately explained the origin of the differences concerning "social distance," they have shown unequivocally that neglect of this factor in human relations or in the design of dwellings and hospitals can have serious social and pathological consequences. The relevance of crowding to mob hysteria and juvenile delinquency is not the less important for having remained so far outside the realm of scientific analysis.

Granted that the pathological consequences of crowding are not yet understood, there is little doubt that they present certain characteristics similar to those associated with other environmental stimuli. In most cases the effects of crowding will be found to have an insidious course, their expressions being determined not so much by the initial effect of the stimulus on a particular target organ, as by the complex secondary responses evoked from the whole organism and from the whole social group.

Civilized life provides a number of social and medical devices that enable modern man to survive, function, and reproduce even though he be crippled, blind, tuberculous, anemic, or endocrinally defective. There is no end in sight to the progress in the biomedical field. It can be anticipated therefore that many new prophylactic and therapeutic procedures will be developed to deal with the health problems created by technological and urban civilization. Medicine is one of the most important aspects of social adaptation to modern life.

Scientific progress, however, is not the only factor of importance in the control of disease. Even assuming that medical science will provide methods of treatment for vascular disorders, malignancies, mental disturbances, and other diseases of civilization, medical control may soon be handicapped by a number of social and economic limitations.

Medical science continues to advance, but the cost of its achievements in the prevention and especially in the treatment of disease becomes higher and higher—not only from the financial point of view, but more importantly with regard to the need for highly specialized skills. For example, heart or lung surgery, artificial kidney dialysis, the treatment of cystic fibrosis or of phenylketonuria, constitute prestigious achievements. But the medical and surgical procedures involved are immensely complex and costly, and they benefit only a very small number of persons.

Unfortunately, the very effectiveness of certain therapeutic procedures is increasing the medical load still further. Patients suffering from genetic diseases now survive—and transmit their genetic defects to their descendants. These in turn will have to be treated for the diseases they have inherited from their parents. Furthermore, the children of persons with genetic defects commonly exhibit an unusually high incidence of congenital abnormalities. This is true even for the children of diabetic women who have been kept under adequate insulin control during pregnancy.

Another type of new problem arises from the fact that increasing numbers of persons are maintained alive by techniques of "medicated survival" which are extremely exacting and costly. The demand for this difficult kind of medical care will become of increasing importance as the population includes a larger percentage of aged persons. Finally, there is the paradoxical fact that some highly effective therapeutic procedures are creating new diseases. For example, man's susceptibility to microorganisms that were not considered pathogenic in the past is commonly increased by administration of antimicrobial drugs, of anticancer agents, of cortisone, as well as by certain forms of surgical intervention.

For all these reasons and many others, medical care will become more and more complex and will demand more and more highly specialized personnel; its cost will inevitably continue to increase. Although hospitalization and modern medical care have become available to a large percentage of the public only during the past few years, some of the economic and social limitations of medicine are already becoming apparent. They will become more severe in the near future.

All over the world, the different countries spend approximately 4 to 6 per cent of their income on medical care irrespective of their wealth. It is probable that there will be social resistance to a further increase of this percentage—and yet medical costs will certainly go up if the burden of disease continues to become heavier, especially if the chronic and degenerative diseases, which require the most complex care, continue their upward trend.

There is already a shortage of physicians and auxiliary medical help even though the present level of medical care is far from adequate. More medical and nursing schools can and will of course be created, but this will be extremely expensive; moreover, the intense competition for talented young people in all professional occupations will inevitably limit the supply of potential qualified applicants. It is very probable that as the numbers of medical and nursing schools continue to increase, the scientific and intellectual quality of training and practice will decrease.

The more advanced the medical procedures, the more they require specialized facilities and personnel. No one can foresee the numbers of persons trained in theoretical biology, chemistry, physics, and engineering that will be required in the future to help physicians carry out the difficult technical procedures that are becoming an essential part of medical practice. In any case, the shortage of ordinary hospital accommodations and of nursing staff is already painfully evident all over the world. Sweden, for example, has found it necessary to buy hospital facilities in Rome (Italy) for the housing of patients suffering from chronic diseases. Furthermore, a Swedish public health officer has estimated that in order to meet the medical requirements of his country, one out of every five able-bodied women would have to engage in nursing work.

In the United States, public and private expenditures in the field of health in 1964 were equivalent to around 6 per cent of the gross national product. The population is increasing faster than the numbers of health workers. The ratio of physicians, nurses, dentists, and other health workers to population is falling precisely at the time when the rise in chronic illness makes higher demands on such specialists as well as on hospital facilities.

It had been assumed a few years ago that, as medical care became more widely available, the demand for it would decrease because the population would become healthier. Unfortunately, the opposite has happened. The pattern of disease is constantly changing and medical care is becoming more exacting.

The greatest improvements in public health have come not from new methods of medical or surgical treatment, but rather from prophylactic measures and other environmental changes. To a very large extent, these improvements have been achieved by eliminating just a few of the most obvious and readily controlled agents of disease. The following changes have probably been among the most influential in the control of disease: greater abundance, quality and variety of food; better clothing, housing, and working conditions; less exacting physical work and more effective protection against inclemencies of the weather; sanitary measures against the spread of gastrointestional infections, in particular, through bacteriological control of water and food; vaccination against smallpox, diphtheria, and a few other infectious diseases; and the ill-defined complex of social practices that brought about a spectacular fall in mortality of tuberculosis long before vaccination or any of the antituberculous drugs were available.

It will be noted that many of the beneficial factors mentioned above correspond to what is generally referred to as "higher living standards." There is no doubt, in fact, that higher living standards have made the population more resistant to various infections and other stresses. But there is reason to fear that we have now reached a phase of diminishing returns in this regard. Furthermore, the high level of prosperity is creating a new set of medical problems. Environmental pollution, excessive food intake, lack of physical exercise, the constant bombardment of stimuli, and the inescapable estrangement of civilized life from the natural biological rhythms are but a few among the many consequences of urbanized and industrialized life that have direct or indirect pathological effects—in particular, the production of vascular, neoplastic, and mental diseases. Environmental pollution in particular seems to be an inevitable result of urbanization of population growth and, paradoxically, of higher living standards. The affluent society is also, as some wags have called it, the "effluent" society.

In brief, it can no longer be taken for granted that a further increase in living standards will result in health improvement. The more probable situation is that it will result in a new pattern of diseases.

One can hope that the factors in our environment that are responsible for the increase in chronic and degenerative diseases will eventually be identified. But even when this has been done it may prove extremely difficult to control the causative factors because all aspects of the urban and industrial environment are so intimately interwoven in the social fabric.

Our societies will have to weigh the dangers arising from new ways of life against the abundance and prosperity derived from technological innovations. It will prove extremely difficult if not impossible to achieve absolute safety, while continuously changing the environment, as is required by progress and economic growth.

The control of the biological environment presents still other difficulties that have their origin in more personal factors.

Keeping streets and houses clear of refuse, filtering and chlorinating the water supplies, watching over the purity of food products, assuring a safe minimum of air in public places, constitute measures that can be applied by the community in an anonymous manner so to speak, and without interfering seriously with individual freedom. These measures do not demand personal effort from their beneficiaries and are therefore readily accepted.

In contrast, any measure that requires individual discipline and effort is more likely to be neglected. Almost everybody is aware of the dangers associated with overeating, failure to engage in physical exercise, chain-smoking of cigarettes, constant exposure to polluted environments and to social stimuli, and excessive consumption of alcohol and of other stimulants or depressants. But few are the persons willing to make the individual and disciplined efforts that would be required to avoid these dangers. Furthermore, the consequences of environmental threats are so often indirect and delayed that the public is hardly aware of them.

In the late nineteenth and the twentieth centuries, public support could be readily gained for action against cholera, typhoid, tuberculosis, venereal diseases, and acute nutritional deficiencies because cause-effect relationship could be made obvious, and the beneficial effect of control measures was almost immediate. In contrast, the evidence linking environmental pollution and objectionable ways of life to chronic and degenerative diseases is at best of a statistical nature; the pathological effects become convincing only when large populations are observed over long periods of time. The public's uncertainty with regard to etiological relationship may account for the failure of the medical profession and of public health services to exhibit zeal in the enforcement of individual or collective control measures.

Fortunately, there is some evidence that the social atmosphere is beginning to change in this regard. The trend is to make the control of environmental pollution a direct responsibility of the industrial producers of pollutants.

In November 1965, a special panel of the President's Science Advisory Committee (PSAC) published a report entitled "Restoring the Quality of our Environment: Report of the Environmental Pollution Panel." The report states at the outset that "Things are bad now but likely to get much worse unless strenuous efforts at improvement are made." It takes the position that ". . . the responsibility of each polluter for all forms of damage caused by his pollution should be effectively recognized and generally accepted. There should be no right to pollute."

It seems worth noting that the report points to the automobile as the most ubiquitous source of pollution in the modern world. It recommends that "the principle of requiring registration before use . . . be extended to the addition to motor fuels of substances which are not eliminated by the combustion process. Widespread use of automobiles has made motor fuels the single most effective way to expose almost all our people to air pollution from combustion-resistant substances such as metals, and as well, to escaped gasoline and combustion products. Lead has long been an additive . . .; phosphorus and boron have been added for a few years; nickel is now beginning to appear."

The report goes so far as to recommend that public funds be expended to support research on a substitute for the internal combustion engine. "We recommend that the Federal government exert every effort to stimulate industry to develop and demonstrate means of powering automobiles and trucks that will not produce noxious effluents. . . . The development of alternative means of mobile energy conversion, suitable for powering automotive transport of all kinds, is not a matter of one year or a few years. Yet if fuel cells, or rechargeable batteries, or other devices are to be developed in time to meet the increased threat, we need to begin now."

While the PSAC panel discussed at length the problems of pesticides, its recommendations were at best vague on this score, and chiefly limited to a plea for fundamental research and education. "Federal support of institutes and centers devoted to research in fields relevant to pollution control is urged and the underwriting of refresher courses and of national and international conferences is recommended." The meaning of the phrase "fundamental research" deserves some discussion at this point.

There is no doubt that, as pointed out in the report, "Disposal of polluting wastes should be the responsibility of those who produce the wastes, and . . . the expense of disposal should be reckoned as part of the cost of doing business." However, implementation of this policy will certainly require complex and costly technological research having little relevance to improvement of the product or to efficiency of plant operation. In other words, it demands a new industrial philosophy.

Attempts must also be made to forecast the potential dangers of social and technological innovations. This will demand complex biological studies, and the resulting financial burden is likely to be large. Society will have to accept the idea that the expenditures involved constitute a legitimate part of research and development cost.

It must be emphasized again in this regard that the pathological effects on man of environmental pollutants and other biologically active substances can be brought to light only through complex and prolonged observations. These observations will have to deal not only with immediate direct effects, but also with those far removed in time from the occurrence of first contact with the substance under consideration. Studies must be directed also to the secondary effects different in mechanism from those corresponding to the initial impact of this substance, and involving structures and functions other than those primarily affected. Man constitutes a complex ecosystem and he responds as an integrated whole to each of the forces that make up his total environment.

Although the PSAC report had undergone scrutiny at the White House, there is little hope that it can have soon a significant influence on pollution control. Maintenance of the present economic and social structure in Western countries is based on the rapid acceptance of technological innovations, in industrial, agricultural, and medical practices. Even granted that earnest efforts will be made to determine beforehand the potential dangers of technological innovations, it would be unrealistic to believe that *all* these dangers can be recognized and avoided.

New techniques and new substances are introduced so rapidly that adequate testing of all of them would paralyze progress. The recent experiences with drug control—a problem far less complex than the control of industrial pollutants—illustrates the magnitude of the difficulties arising from any attempt at formulating strict safety regulations. It takes more than people, time, money, or laboratory and office facilities, to determine the potential dangers of technological innovations. It takes a kind of theoretical knowledge that does not exist and is not vigorously pursued. However strict the safety regulations, and however diligent the work of those who try to apply them, accidents will happen because the theoretical basis of toxicology is not sufficiently developed to permit a prediction of dangers to health. Let it be mentioned in passing that environmental medicine constitutes a field of knowledge almost completely neglected at the present time, and that would deserve large-scale support from foundations concerned with pioneering studies in social development.

Since there is no progress without risks, it appears at first sight that the rapid development of new techniques and new products implies the immolation of mankind to a technology gone wild. But the future need not be as dark as that. We must abandon, it is true, the utopian concept that safety regulations can protect us completely from threats to health in the modern world, but this does not mean accepting passively the consequences of such dangers.

In addition to gaining advance theoretical knowledge of the biological effects of new substances and new techniques, it is urgent to develop epidemiological techniques for recognizing as soon as possible manifestations of toxicity in the population at large. Early recognition would help in identifying the technological and social changes that constitute threats to health. This approach, which might be termed prospective epidemiology, is one of the steps in the process of continuous self-correction, without which scientific knowledge cannot make a lasting contribution to health improvement.

Health surveys such as the one now being conducted on a national scale by the United States Public Health Service will provide useful data for the recognition of new pathological states associated with the modern ways of life. But such surveys are so ponderous that they cannot detect early enough the new dangers to public health. They should be supplemented by an elaborate system of listening posts that would enable public health authorities to recognize signs of abnormality in the population, and to organize rapidly more pointed epidemiological surveys as needed. To a limited extent this is being done for detecting resistance of pathogens or of their vectors to antimicrobial drugs or to insecticides. Largely as a result of the impetus provided by the thalidomide episode, the World Health Organization has initiated such a campaign for the development of a worldwide warning system for toxic effects of drugs under a resolution passed in May, 1963, at the Sixteenth World Health Assembly. In the United States the Food and Drug Administration is supporting this program as a first step toward an international drug safeguard plan.

A number of physiological, chemical, and hematological tests could certainly be devised to detect abnormalities in human populations and thus broaden the coverage of potential threats to health. What is proposed here is that the kind of prospective epidemiology that is being carried out at present in an episodic manner to deal with special situations should become more systematic and constitute a continuous part of social management in industrialized societies. The aim would be early containment of new threats to health, rather than the utopian goal of complete prevention or eradication of disease.

The development of a social sense of alertness to the inevitable dangers of technological innovations is part of the social adaptive process to the conditions of the modern world. Prospective epidemiology could be regarded as a kind of social protective organ, at least as essential to disease control as are the safety regulations by which official agencies attempt to protect the public against unforeseeable dangers.

Unfortunately, epidemiological surveys have the great drawback that they commonly yield the needed information too late for the development of corrective measures. In the case of environmental pollution, especially, the situation may well become unmanageable if the accumulation of convincing epidemiological evidence is made a prerequisite of social action. Furthermore, it is usually difficult to prove convincingly the role of any given pollutant in the causation of disease. While much basic epidemiological and pathological research is needed in this field, action must be taken now lest disasters overtake us.

In the words of the PSAC report mentioned above, "We now know that the full effects of environmental changes produced by pollution cannot be foreseen before judgments must be made. The responsible judgment therefore must be the conservative one. Trends and indications, as soundly based as possible, must provide the guidelines; demonstration of disaster is not required. Abnormal changes in animal populations, however small, at whatever stage in the life history of the individual, or in whatever niche of the species complex, must be considered warnings of potential hazard."

Fortunately, several types of physiological tests in man and of experimental studies in animals can be devised to demonstrate that many pollutants have adverse effects on essential structures and functions. Such tests and studies cannot entirely substitute for epidemiological surveys because they are not likely to reveal *all* the potential dangers of environmental pollution. But they have the advantage of providing rapidly a type of information which is readily measurable and therefore likely to be more convincing than that derived from statistical epidemiology. A kind of knowledge that is striking even though incomplete is here of great psychological importance. Environmental pollution will not be controlled until physicians and scientists take an active part in its study and until the general public is alerted to the dangers of the "pestilence that walketh in darkness." The threats to health posed by environmental pollution are so great that in many cases action must be taken before all evidence is at hand. Academic purism is a virtue within the university; in the practical world, however, it often becomes an escape from social responsibility and a form of intellectual abdication.

The foregoing discussion has dealt exclusively with the pathological effects of the environment, considered from the traditional point of view of the public health sciences. But it is obvious that environmental factors condition man's welfare in many other ways. The formulation of an ideal environment should take into consideration all aspects of man's life including his emotional needs and the development of his civilizations.

Any discussion of man's fundamental nature and needs must start from the fact that the evolution of *Homo sapiens* had been essentially completed some 100,000 years ago. One could almost say indeed that mankind was created with all its fundamental characteristics, potentialities, and limitations during the late Paleolithic period when the genetic code of *Homo sapiens* achieved its present formula.

Awareness of the permanency of man's nature is important for the management of modern life. Just as modern man retains useless anatomic vestiges of his distant evolutionary past, so he has inherited several of the patterns of physiological and emotional responses that primitive man had developed when he had to face the forces of nature without help. The chemical and hormonal activities of man's body are still geared to the movements of the earth around the sun and of the moon around the earth, even under the most urbanized conditions of modern life. Likewise, many emotional and hormonal responses are still conditioned by the patterns of response developed during prehistoric times. This survival of the biological past affects most experiences of the human condition under present circumstances, in health as well as in disease.

The weekend exodus to the country, pathetic as it is in its present form, symbolizes man's biological need to retain some contact with "nature." While the medieval and Renaissance city was perhaps as crowded as the modern city, its inhabitants were not completely separated from nature because fields, forests, and streams were readily accessible within a short walking distance outside its walls.

Because man's biological evolution has now come almost to a standstill, and will be slowed down still further by the inevitable restrictions in family size, there are definite limits to his adaptive potentialities. Furthermore, there is no chance that his genetic endowment can be safely or usefully modified during the foreseeable future—if ever. It is essential therefore to keep in mind the biological limitations of *Homo sapiens* when considering the extent to which the ways of life and the environment can be transformed by technology. Technological civilization can survive only if it takes cognizance of the fundamental biological attributes of mankind which are essentially unchangeable. Our chief concern should be not the frontiers of scientific technology but the unchangeable characteristics and the frontiers of man.

Many unproven assumptions, furthermore, underlie the belief that the goal of technology, including medicine, should be to provide man with a sheltered environment in which he is protected as completely as possible from any form of traumatic experience. This assumption is dangerous because certain important traits of man's nature cannot develop normally, or remain in a healthy state, without constant stimulation and challenge. Life at constant temperature through air conditioning, learning made effortless through mechanical aids, avoidance of conflicts through social adjustment, are examples of the means by which modern life eliminates or minimizes physiological or psychological effort, but by the same token results in atrophy of man's adaptive mechanisms. While protection from stresses and from effort may add to the pleasure or at least to the comfort of the moment, and while emotional neutrality minimizes social conflicts, the consequences of an excessively sheltered life are certainly unfavorable in the long run. They are even dangerous in that man becomes adjusted to a particular place and time, but loses his ability to readjust as surroundings change.

Uniformity of social and technological conditions indirectly brings about other types of undesirable effects. If the social and technological environment is so narrow as to favor the development of only a few human traits, the ones that are repressed tend to be eliminated gradually, at least in their phenotypic expression. The creeping monotony of our technological culture goes hand in hand with the monotony of our patterns of education, behavior, taste, and mass communication. It is high time that we make a deliberate effort to create and maintain as diversified an environment as possible, even though this results in some loss of efficiency, in order to provide the many kinds of soil needed for the germination of the seeds now dormant in man's nature. Diversity in social environment should be made one of the crucial tests of true functionalism, whether in the planning of cities, the design of dwellings, or the management of life experiences. A highly structured and unified environment may be desirable for the sake of order, efficiency, and peace. But diversification of the environment is needed to bring out the unexpressed potentialities of mankind, and allow the unfolding of civilizations.

Leonard J. Duhl

⸨ MENTAL HEALTH IN AN ⸩
⸨ URBAN SOCIETY ⸩

René Dubos is one of the really great teachers in the field of medicine. In fact, he is more than a teacher; he is an agent of change who forces us to look at problems we have taken for granted, and at traditional methods of coping with them, in an entirely new light.

His paper reflects concerns that I have had for a long time. In my own field—that of psychiatry—primary concern has been with treatment, with hospitals, and with clinics. If one is interested in people in the mass and wishes, as I did, to go into the area of prevention, he has to step far out of that world of psychiatry—the psychiatric hospital, and even the laboratory—and deal with problems of city planning and law; of economics and other social sciences; of geography and even some of the natural sciences. All this is perplexing; and the really difficult problem is to put these scattered bits together in some kind of ecological or systems model. It is much easier psychologically to cut up man into many separate parts, or to divide the environment into many different segments, than to pull them together into some kind of ecological whole, whether it is the ecology of the natural environment or the ecology of the urban environment that man has created for himself.

Wholeness, the comprehension of the totality of things, is a very

Leonard J. Duhl *is a psychiatrist with a long-standing interest in problems of the urban environment. Since March 1966 he has been senior consultant to the Secretary of Housing and Urban Development. For a dozen years before that he was on the staff of the National Institute of Mental Health, where his last position was Chief, Office of Planning. Editor of three books, including* The Urban Condition: People and Policy in the Metropolis, *he is also the author of numerous papers for journals or symposia and was a contributor to an earlier RFF Forum, which resulted in the 1963 volume* Cities and Space. *Dr. Duhl was born in New York City in 1926. He received his A.B. degree from Columbia University, his M.D. from Albany Medical College, and was a fellow at the Menninger Foundation School of Psychiatry.*

unsteady state. No matter where we are, whether in a psychiatric hospital or an office concerned with the problems of the city, if we stop our vigil just one moment we all too often retreat to the simpler things that we can see, can measure neatly and understand clearly and put together in a very rational, systematic way. But, unfortunately, those parts that are fuzzy, that we don't understand and can't analyze, probably have more impact on our total life than all those nice, neat things that we can study.

Thus, I think that Dr. Dubos is primarily concerned in his paper with the way of looking at problems and that this accounts for his concern with beginning to act now, before we have all the knowledge that is necessary to be completely rational and to understand what the issues are.

At the present time I am in the process of shifting jobs, from the National Institute of Mental Health to the Department of Housing and Urban Development. In doing so, I am moving into an area with which I have long been concerned, but it is not always easy to link up my old concerns with the performance of the whole human being—the way he copes, the way he breaks down, and the way he adapts to the design of our cities and our urban centers. When we look at the urban world (which already is the world of the majority of Americans, and the trend still is running strongly) we see that all the solutions up to now have been segmented. We have talked about buildings, we have talked about parks, we have talked about transportation, and we have talked about hospitals. But all you have to do is grope your way through the legislation of the United States government and then look at the way the laws are carried out, and you see how disconnected all the programs are. They are not connected in any way, either in concept or in specification or in the groups of people who are given the responsibility to do something about the problems.

I have a feeling we are at a point which Sir Geoffrey Vickers calls "the end of free fall." He tells a story of a man who jumped off the Empire State Building; as he passes the second floor, he says, "Well, at least I am still alive now." We in urbanized America are past that stage where we can say this. We are suddenly entering an era in which for the first time we are going to have to think differently, create our institutions differently, our research differently. Activities will have to be oriented in new patterns around the complex interrelationships of professions and disciplines and ways of behaving.

I think that there will have to be many new research institutes and many innovations in the training of professionals. We are going to have to find people familiar with the linkages between the professions—people who can tie things together, not in the beautiful systematic way of some of the systems theorists, but sometimes in the loose, open, flexible way that Gilbert White describes later in this book.

This complexity is being forced on us for many reasons. A psychiatric reason is that we are suddenly at that point in time where all the input of information, of ideas, of conflicting values, of aspirations, and what-have-you is pounding in on us, and the individual is faced with a tremendously difficult problem of how to put this together and how to find some identity from it, and I don't think we can any longer be in the position of asking any individual or even any one institution to take all this tremendous diverse input and put it together. A number of institutions will have to be created to put this information together for us in a different way and we will have to train professionals that will help with the process of integration.

But in all this, there is a frightening possibility that if one tries to put pieces together in a very rational and logical way, as many of the systems theorists are doing it, somehow people get left behind. In the hierarchy of values that we utilize in making decisions, all sorts of things come before the concern with the human being. Perhaps this is because, as Dr. Dubos has indicated, the effects on human beings take much longer periods of time to show themselves than some of these other concrete things that can be noted and measured within a year or two. Perhaps the problem is even more complicated than that; it may have something to do with the fact that we really don't value ourselves as much as we say we do, and that we are willing to sacrifice ourselves for all the new technology and for our fantastic aspirations. If so, we pay a price.

In the modern city—in the United States and all over the world—there are many people who, because of the tremendous input of information from everywhere, have increased their aspirations multifold. They, too, would like all the things that we are selling. But their ability and their skill to achieve these aspirations are very minimal. And yet some of them are flexing their muscles and some of them are beginning to make themselves heard. Some make themselves heard in the fluoridation battles and some make themselves heard in the civil rights movement. But I suggest that in a very, very short time, almost all the things of environmental concern today, and those that are being talked about in medicine or in urban affairs or in education, are going to be affected by the fact that the consumer, the nonprofessional, the man who really doesn't know the issues, is going to start to say what he really wants and is going to have a tremendous impact.

I don't know whether he wants wholeness, as I indicated, but I think he had better. And even though the general public opinion polls don't show that this is considered necessary, I believe that the responsibility of leadership is the responsibility of putting things together and of laying out a complex program over the years to come. I am not thinking of omnibus bills, with a little of everything in them, but of a coherent program—that might be called ecological planning—with priorities, with a period of time, say twenty-five to thirty-five years. Then we could begin to set our sights not only for research, but for the training of some of the manpower that will be so desperately needed.

Chapter Three

❧ BEYOND THE MARKET MECHANISM ❧

Ralph Turvey

SIDE EFFECTS OF RESOURCE USE

Many of the problems with which this book is concerned involve some sort of failure of the market mechanism as it now functions. The failure arises because decisions concerning the use of natural resources do not always take into account all the effects of that use. The neglected or side effects on the quality of the environment can, however, be very important, and thus need examination.

My purpose here is not to list and evaluate such side effects. It is the more limited one of analyzing their nature and introducing the various possible ways of coping with them. Economists have thought about all this and have produced an extensive and fairly technical literature on the subject. I have endeavored to distill from it the main ideas that are relevant to this volume and to present them in practical terms. Although I shall try to minimize the amount of jargon, I had better begin by stating that the technical terms used include "side-use effects," "spillovers," "externalities" or "external economies and diseconomies." These can be roughly and generally defined as the impacts of the activities of households, public agencies, or enterprises upon the activities of other households, public agencies, or enterprises which are exerted otherwise than through the market. They are, in other words, relationships other than those between buyer and seller.

Ralph Turvey *is Chief Economist of Britain's Electricity Council, a public organization with headquarters in London. Formerly he was Reader in Economics with special reference to public finance, at the London School of Economics. His publications include* The Economics of Real Property, Interest Rates and Asset Prices, *and (with George Break)* Studies in Greek Taxation. *He has been visiting professor at several universities in the United States, including Chicago and Johns Hopkins, and was seconded to the Economic Section of the U.K. Treasury for two years. Mr. Turvey was born in Birmingham in 1927. He received his B.Sc. (economics) from the London School of Economics in 1947 and did graduate work at the University of Uppsala in Sweden.*

To make this notion clearer it is best to proceed directly to the examples that I shall use. All seven of them are significant in practice. But it is important to note that they are used only as illustrations and that I do not pretend to deal fully with any of them.

Fisheries constitute the first example. In some kinds of fisheries, once a certain intensity of fishing is reached, the stock of fish is reduced with the result that fishing is made more difficult and costly. This means that each fisherman, by taking fish, is adding to the costs of all the other fishermen. What is more, not only the scale of the activity, as measured by the weight of fish caught, but also its nature is relevant, since (in a trawl fishery) the mesh size of the nets used also affects the stock. An increase in mesh size, by raising the minimum size of fish caught, would in some fisheries ultimately result in an increase in the stock, so making fishing easier. Thus by using a smaller mesh instead of a larger one, each fisherman is raising the costs of all the other fishermen.

In this example the impact of each fisherman's activity upon that of others is reciprocal. This feature is shared with the next two examples while, as we shall see, this is not the case with the last four of our seven examples, where the impact of one activity upon another is unidirectional.

The second example consists of traffic congestion on roads or in an urban street network. Once traffic flow exceeds a certain level, vehicles (and pedestrians) get in each others' way and slow down the traffic flow. Thus any one vehicle affects other vehicles by increasing the time spent and the fuel used in the journeys which those other vehicles are making. The relationship is reciprocal because the presence of each vehicle adds to the costs of all the others.

The same is true of the third example: wells which all tap a common source of water. Each well deprives other wells of some water, either by reducing their rate of flow or by bringing nearer the day when their yield diminishes.

Reciprocality is not the only common feature of these three examples. They are also alike in that, usually at least, a large number of households or enterprises are involved: hundreds of fishermen, thousands of vehicles and dozens of wells. These two features are not logically connected, of course, but just happen to be common to these three examples. Now this raises an expositional question which it may be as well to get out of the way before we go on. The tidy minded, seeing that different examples have different combinations of features, will call for the taxonomy of all possible types of cases which could be produced by classifying and cross-classifying all possible relevant features. Even if I am accused of not being tidy minded, however, I am not going to do this, partly because it is boring and partly because so many of the pigeonholes thus created would remain empty for lack of a corresponding real case.[1]

Continuing, then, by enumerating real examples, my other cases are unidirectional. The fourth is the adverse effect upon households living round an airport of the noise of jets landing and taking off; the fifth is river pollution by the discharge of industrial effluents,[2] and the sixth is the destruction of visual amenity involved in placing overhead power transmission lines in areas of scenic beauty.

Seventh, and last, is cattle poisoning by the emission of fluorine in the smoke from brickworks. Fluorosis causes cows' teeth to mottle and wear faster than normal. Their bones grow deformed and brittle and may break. The consequence is that milk yields and the values of the animals drop considerably; cows may even have to be slaughtered.

We can now use our examples to show that where side effects—externalities—are involved in resource use, the market mechanism, i.e., buyer-seller relationships, alone may not produce the best possible allocation of resources. Some additional mechanism may produce a better allocation of resources by causing households or firms to alter the scales or the nature of their activities.

This is a rather general statement, so I must use my examples to show what it means. But there is another general statement to make first: the right word is "may" not "will." We should never aim to get rid of absolutely all external effects of one activity upon another, since the net gain from doing so would be negative. A world with no traffic congestion at all, never any noise, no overhead power lines and not a trace of smoke is a nice thought, but irrelevant to action. Thus the question is not one of abolishing adverse unfavorable effects, but is one of reducing them in some cases where investigation shows that on balance such a reduction is worthwhile.

Let us now list the main activity adjustments that are possible in the seven examples. First, fishing. Here a reduction in the amount of fishing

---

[1] One economist, E. J. Mishan, in an otherwise useful article on the theory of the subject, "Reflections on Recent Developments in the Concept of External Effects" (*Canadian Journal of Economics and Political Science,* February 1965), solemnly suggests a certain fourfold classification as being "useful" which he can only fill with such examples as: "a project for a single giant airliner the vibration from which made it impossible to operate a pottery industry."

[2] Allen V. Kneese and Resources for the Future have provided us with such a first-rate book on water pollution, *The Economics of Regional Water Quality Management* (Baltimore: The Johns Hopkins Press, 1964), that I feel justified in treating this particular example fairly cavalierly in this paper.

effort and an increase in mesh size will first lower the catch and then raise it and/or make possible a further reduction in the amount of fishing effort. Thus there is an initial loss, in that fewer fish are caught, followed by a continuing gain, in that the catch will rise more or fall less[3] than the number of boats and men engaged in the fishery. In either case, cost per ton of fish caught will end up lower than it was to start with.

Second, roads. A reduction in the number of vehicles would reduce the time and running costs incurred in the journeys of the remaining vehicles. Similarly, a reduction in the amount of on-street parking is a nuisance for the drivers who wish to park but will benefit moving traffic (and pedestrians).

Third, wells. If fewer wells were drilled, drilling costs would be saved while the off-take of water would be reduced less.

Fourth, aircraft noise. In unidirectional cases, such as this, there is usually scope for both the creator of the adverse external effect and the sufferer from it to adjust the scale and the nature of their activity. Thus airlines can reduce the number of night jet take-offs, modify engines to reduce noise and alter the speed and angle of ascent—all at a cost. The households around the airport, on the other hand, can install sound-proofing or move.

Fifth, the emission of effluent into rivers. The enterprise or sewerage authority can treat the effluent before discharging it and possibly install storage facilities in order to reduce the rate of discharge at times when the river is low. In some cases an enterprise can also alter its production process in order to reduce the noxiousness of its effluent or it can even shift its location. Those enterprises or public authorities downstream can also spend money on treating the polluted river water in order to reduce the adverse consequences of the pollution and households can move.

Sixth, power lines. These can be sited differently or put underground.

Seventh, brickworks. Smoke filtering is possible and so is a change of location—two very expensive alternatives. Farmers, on the other hand, can shift from dairy farming to poultry or arable farming.

This review of the examples shows that there are frequently several possible ways in which the nature or scale of activities can be modified in order to reduce the adverse consequences of external effects. In most actual cases, therefore, the problem is a multidimensional one: who should do what how much?

---

[3] This is a little complicated. I have analyzed the problem and provided references to the literature in my paper "Optimization and Suboptimization in Fishery Regulation" (*American Economic Review,* March 1964).

Ralph Turvey 51

An economic criterion can be used in answering this question. It is simply that the present value of the monetary measure of all gains from modifying activities less the present value of the monetary measure of all losses from these modifications be maximized. Unfortunately, this test is rarely sufficient in itself to provide an answer, and often cannot be applied in practice.

Nobody is going to quarrel with this criterion as a principle; it is like being against sin! But it is able to give an answer only when all gains and all losses can be satisfactorily measured and expressed in terms of a common denominator, dollars. Gains and losses occurring at different times are rendered comparable by using a discount rate which expresses one's evaluation of futurity to turn them into their equivalent gains and losses at a common reference date. Given satisfactory measurement, given expression in dollar terms and given an agreed discount rate, to apply the criterion is to choose the best.

The beauty of this criterion, in the eyes of some economists, is that whenever its application indicates that some course of action is desirable—gains exceed losses—the gainers can fully compensate the losers and still remain better off. Thus nobody loses on balance and at least some of the parties end up better off. What can be fairer than that?

The answer is that payment of compensation by gainers to losers is not always considered fair, so that even if it were always practicable it would not always be done. Yet the idea which lies at the root of the criterion (namely, that a course of action can be regarded unequivocally as desirable if it makes some people better off and nobody worse off) requires that compensation actually be paid.

The brickworks example can be used to illustrate this, if we take it that all that matters are brick costs and farming costs and sales, all of them measurable in monetary terms. Suppose (though it is probably not true at present) that application of the criterion showed the best course of action to be cleansing brickwork smoke.[4] This would mean that the gain to farmers from an improvement in the health of any cows they keep would exceed the cost to the brickworks of cleansing the smoke, so that farmers could fully compensate the brickworks and yet remain net gainers. My point is that many people would not regard it as fair to make the farmers compensate the brickworks; on the contrary, they would claim that fairness requires the brickworks to meet the cost of cleansing the smoke since the brickworks is responsible for the damage.

Let us accept this judgment. Then the introduction of smoke cleansing

[4] According to a report in *The Times* of London (May 5, 1965), a scheme for cleansing brickwork smoke which uses a wet scrubber and heat exchanger would put up the cost of bricks by 25 per cent.

will not make some people better off and nobody worse off; instead it will harm the brickworks and benefit the farmers. Thus, in deciding whether or not the smoke ought to be cleansed, we are not just comparing total gains with total losses; we are also deciding whether or not it is fair to impose a loss on the brickworks.

What this example shows, then, is that even when all gains and losses can be measured and rendered comparable by expressing them in dollar terms, the economic criterion taken by itself is not always sufficient for choosing the right course of action. Considerations of fairness may also be relevant. In a democratic country this means that the problem may have a political aspect.

When some of the gains and losses cannot be expressed in dollar terms, the choice of the right course of action always has a political aspect, for it always involves judgments about fairness as well as mere calculation. The airport example illustrates this. The cost to airlines of reducing noise and the cost to householders of soundproofing their dwellings can no doubt be calculated in monetary terms. But the gain to householders from a reduction in noise cannot.[5] Hence deciding what measures, if any, should be taken involves:

> ascertaining the cheapest way of achieving various reductions in noise levels;
> choosing the reduction to aim at;
> deciding who should bear the cost;

and the two latter issues, which are interdependent, both involve judgments of fairness or what I am here calling political considerations.

All this goes to show, then, that who should do what how much is often a question which cannot be decided on a purely technical basis by an economic calculation. Political considerations—judgments of what is equitable—are also required. This is the message for economists and technologists. On the other hand, there also is a message for administrators and politicians; namely, that even though an economic calculation of gains and losses is often not sufficient to reach a well based decision, it is nearly always an essential preliminary.

We are now ready to go on to discuss possible mechanisms for dealing with external effects. Since these, by definition, are relationships which are not co-ordinated by the market mechanism, it is a truism to say that these mechanisms are either nonmarket ones or that they involve the

---

[5] Asking people how much they would pay to obtain a given reduction in noise and comparing the prices of similar houses near and remote from the airport are both impracticable.

creation of a market where none existed before, i.e., the creation of rights which can be bought and sold. These are like the classical alternatives of status or contract.

Regulation is the mechanism of most general appeal, at least to noneconomists. It is easy to find examples:

Specification of a minimum mesh size to be used in a fishery;

Prohibition of parking at certain times in certain streets;

Confining the use of water from wells to certain purposes;

Limitation of the number of night take-offs by jet planes;

Requiring that effluents be treated before discharge into a river;

Forbidding the erection of overhead power lines in areas of natural beauty;

Prohibition of brickworks in certain areas (zoning).

Regulation may either consist of general rules or of specific decisions on individual cases. A good example of the latter is furnished by the British treatment of overhead power lines. The Central Electricity Generating Board, which is responsible for the National Grid, has a statutory responsibility to consider the impact of its activities upon amenity and has to get a statutory consent from the Minister of Power for each new transmission line.

The Board's earliest approaches are to the County Planning Officers and to bodies such as the Service Departments, National Parks Commission and Nature Conservancy. With their help a route is gradually evolved that can be formally submitted for consideration by all the local authorities and county councils it affects. Often—indeed, with a majority of lines—the approval of the local authorities is forthcoming at once when this form of submission is made, thanks to the consultations that have taken place earlier. On the other hand, it may be that a local authority wants some alteration in the route. This will be looked into by the Board and if acceptable a fresh submission made. Or, as must sometimes happen, the Board may in the end have to say that it is unable to suggest a route that would meet with the authority's approval.

Having taken negotiations with local authorities as far as practicable, the Board then applies for the statutory consent and, with it, for planning permission. For these an application is made to the Ministry of Power to whom the Board sends on the observations it has had in response to its submissions to the county councils and local authorities. At this point of time the Board has to give publicity to its proposals by advertising in local newspapers, stating where plans of the route can be examined. In this way members of the public are given an opportunity to find out what is proposed and, if they want, to lodge an objection with the Minister of

Power. If there are no objections at this stage, and if the route has been approved by the local authorities and county councils, the Minister's consent (with planning permission) can be expected without more ado. But if there are serious objections from any quarter, public or private, the Minister will arrange for a public inquiry or hearing to take place at which both the Board and the objectors will argue their cases in front of an inspector appointed by the Minister. When amenity issues are involved the inspector may be accompanied by another inspector from the Ministry of Housing and Local Government. After the inquiry the inspector makes a report, in the light of which the Minister decides whether to give consent or to reject the Board's application.[6]

It is scarcely necessary to say that regulation of one sort or another is often the most appropriate way of dealing with external effects. What does need saying, however, is that this is not always true: sometimes the cure is worse than the disease and sometimes other mechanisms of control are better. I do not believe that any general classification can be provided to tell us what is best in any particular case; on the contrary, I think that each case must be examined in some detail. My task is therefore to show by example what alternatives there are and to indicate the circumstances under which they may be feasible.

The first alternative involves creating a contract between the parties. If B carries on an activity which damages A, A can offer to pay B some money in consideration of his reducing the scale or changing the nature of his activity in order to diminish or abolish the damage. Such a bargain will be mutually advantageous when the economic criterion discussed above is fulfilled. If some alteration of B's activity costs B less than it profits A, the latter can afford to pay B enough to meet these costs. Thus suppose that an expenditure of $1,000 by B is worth $1,500 to A. Then if A pays B anything between $1,001 and $1,499, B will gain something between one dollar and $499 and A will gain between $499 and one dollar.

When the point is put in these abstract terms it invites the response that this sort of bargaining is open to blackmailers. Might not B be tempted to bother A solely in order to turn a dishonest penny by getting A to pay him to stop? The answer is, of course, that the parties must act within a legal framework of rights and obligations which determines their bargaining positions. The law of nuisance is particularly relevant here, both because it is an important part of this framework and because

---

[6] This and the previous paragraph are taken almost verbatim from a brochure *Pattern of Power* issued by the Central Electricity Generating Board, London, 1963.

it provides a second alternative to the sort of regulations listed above; namely, the award of injunctions by the courts.

Nuisances, in the legal sense, are acts not warranted by law (or failure to discharge legal duties) which obstruct, inconvenience or damage the public or which, when concerned with the use or occupation of land, damage another person in connection with his occupation or use of land. This latter category constitutes private nuisance and it is only here that a private individual has a right to legal action and may claim damages or an injunction. Whether an act constitutes a nuisance is a matter either of common law or of statute; thus the Public Health Acts specify a number of statutory nuisances where legal proceedings are initiated by public authorities. It is important to note that some acts which would otherwise be wrongful may be authorized by statute. Thus actions for nuisance arising from civil aircraft are prohibited.

The law of nuisance may, however, apply to another of our examples. Certain farmers are taking legal proceedings with the object of obtaining redress for the loss and damage which their farms have suffered due to fluorine. (They are not seeking an injunction; in the case of brickworks because it is not practicable to eliminate the fluorine from the emissions.) An alternative method which has actually been used in one or two cases is for the manufacturer to purchase an affected farm on such terms as to avoid claims in respect of fluorine pollution.

Leaving aside the technical point, yet to be resolved, as to whether damage can be proved to the satisfaction of the courts, this case shows that if the farmers have a right, their bargaining position will be improved. An alternative to payment of damages is a private contract which avoids claims for damages. In this particular case it appears that the cost (to brickworks) of ceasing to emit fluorine exceeds the cost (to farmers) imposed by its continued emission. Thus the economic criterion suggests that the right thing is for the emission to continue, whether or not the farmers have a right against the brickworks. If they do not have such a right, they bear the cost. If they do, the brickworks bears the cost either in the form of damages awarded by the courts or by payment made under a contract. Thus the absence or existence of the right on the part of the farmers does not affect the allocation of resources between activities but only the distribution of the gains and losses between the parties.[7] The law of nuisance is thus only relevant to the fairness of what happens.

[7] For a rigorous exposition, see my expository paper "On Divergences Between Social Cost and Private Cost" (*Economica,* August 1963). The point was made in Professor Coase's important paper "The Problem of Social Cost" (*Journal of Law and Economics,* October 1960).

Whether or not this result follows in all cases where the parties can make a private bargain is difficult to say.[8] It is easy to imagine circumstances in which civil proceedings might fail to lead to the maximization of net gains, particularly since in British law it is no defense for the person committing a nuisance to prove that the benefit to the public far exceeds the disadvantage!

An actual river-pollution case will serve to illustrate the complexities of the problem and to show why generalization is difficult. This is the Pride of Derby Angling Association and the Earl of Harrington versus Derby Corporation, British Celanese Ltd. and the British Electricity Authority.[9] The plaintiffs' waters had been polluted and the water temperature had been raised, with injurious results to fish, by the discharge of heated trade effluent by British Celanese, by the discharge of insufficiently treated sewage matter by Derby Corporation and by the discharge of heated water by the (then) British Electricity Authority. An injunction was granted but was suspended for two years to give the defendants time to remedy matters; meanwhile the defendants had to indemnify the plaintiff against the damage.

Three features of this case are of particular interest. The first is that since the two plaintiffs' waters had been polluted by the combined effects of the activities of the defendants, they were entitled to bring an action against all three of them. The second emerges from the following statement made by Lord Evershed in the course of his judgment on the appeal:

> It is, I think, well settled that if A proves that his proprietary rights are being wrongfully interfered with by B, and that B intends to continue his wrong, than A is prima facie entitled to an injunction, and he will be deprived of that remedy only if special circumstances exist, including the circumstance that damages are an adequate remedy for the wrong that he

[8] It is as well to mention that one can conceive of conditions when the structure of rights *will* affect resource allocation. If B's activity damages A, the maximum amount which A would pay B to modify his activity may be less than the minimum amount which he would accept from B to compensate him for continuing to tolerate the activity unmodified. In these circumstances A might be unable to reach an agreement with B requiring B to modify his activity when he had no rights against B, yet be able to reach an agreement if he did have such rights. Alternatively, a similar result might occur because of a difference between the minimum amount he would pay in order to avoid having to modify it.

This complication is a tribute to the ability of economic theorists to refine their analyses but it is difficult to see that it will be important save when *either* A is a person, is poor and is severely damaged, *and/or* B is a person, is poor and would find the modification very expensive.

[9] "All England Law Reports," 1952 Vol. 1 and, on Appeal, 1953 Vol. 1. An important issue which need not be discussed here was whether or not the Corporation and the Authority had statutory defense.

has suffered. In the present case it is plain that damages would be a wholly inadequate remedy for the first-named plaintiffs, who have not been incorporated in order to fish for monthly sums.

Since there was apparently no inquiry into the costs to the defendants of ceasing to pollute one may be forgiven for wondering whether it is clear that gains less losses were maximized.

The third interesting feature of this case is that the interests of the fishermen were looked after by their Angling Association, a voluntary collective body formed precisely for purposes such as this. Economists tend to neglect such voluntary associations, concentrating instead on compulsory associations for collective action—the public authorities. Yet their function is similar: to do collectively what cannot be done by the market or by bargains between individuals.

The public authorities are, of course, able to pursue courses of action which are not open to voluntary associations. They can bring proceedings in respect of public nuisances. Another way, already mentioned, is by regulation—either general or particular. But there is yet a third way, not mentioned so far, which has long interested economists. This is the use of special taxes. The argument runs as follows: If group B's activity adversely affects group A, this means that group B is imposing a cost upon group A so that the cost to society as a whole of group B's activity (its social cost) exceeds its cost to group B itself (its private cost). Thus in looking only at its private cost when deciding upon its activity, group B must fail to maximize the excess of gains over social cost. It can be induced to take social cost rather than private cost into account, however, if it is charged a tax which raises its private cost to equality with social cost. Thus an external diseconomy is viewed as an excess of social over private cost and is to be dealt with by levying a tax equal to this excess.

We have earlier seen how a nonoptimal situation where a single B adversely affects a single A can usually be remedied either if A is able to secure adequate but not excessive damages from B (when he has a right against him) or by his paying B to desist (when he has not). In just the same way, a tax imposed by the public authorities upon a group B could be replaced by the public authorities paying group B to desist. The same allocation of resources can usually be achieved in either case; the difference is thus in most cases only a question of fairness, i.e., of the distribution of the costs and gains between group B on the one hand and the public authority's taxpayers on the other.

Fishery regulation, street congestion, and the use of water from wells are all examples in which economists have urged that a properly designed tax would be superior to any form of regulation. Actually, some combination of both is probably required. Thus, in the case of fish, it can be shown[10] that a tax on catch should be accompanied by regulation of mesh size if the present value of gains minus losses is to be maximized.

The external diseconomies in these three examples are reciprocal. Reflection suggests that this is because all three involve what economists call a common property resource. This is a resource required in production which is significantly limited in availability but whose use is nonetheless free. In the three examples this resource is, respectively, the fish stock, the street system, and the underground water. An increase in the catch, the number of journeys undertaken, and the amount of water abstracted lowers the fish stock, increases street congestion, and reduces water reserves. This raises the costs of all fishermen, all drivers, and all water users by making fish more difficult to catch, slowing down traffic, and lowering the water table. But this effect of an increase in the use of the common property resource by one user is not felt by him; it is felt by his fellows. Thus the social cost of any given increase in the catch, vehicle-miles, or gallons exceeds the private cost of such an increase to the one who provides it. By using up more of the common property resource he leaves less of it for his fellows; this is a cost but it is a social cost only and not a private cost as well because he does not pay for its use. Putting a price on the use of the common property resource, however, could raise private cost to equality with social cost and put an end to the wasteful and excessively intensive use of the common property resource. It is wastefully used because it is free to the user but significantly scarce; it is treated like air but is really like good agricultural land.

This last paragraph aims to set out the essentials of the matter, not to provide a rigorous demonstration. It suffices here to point out that agricultural land would be wastefully exploited if farmers could all use it without buying or renting it—as indeed happens sometimes with common land. Thus the proceeds to be got from a properly designed tax on catch, urban road journeys, or water abstraction constitute the rent which society as a whole could obtain from better utilization of its common property resource.[11]

Urban roads differ from the other two examples in that the amount available is entirely within the control of man. But this does not affect

---

[10] See my paper in the *American Economic Review* cited earlier.

[11] This is less than the maximum profit which would be obtained by a monopolist owner of the resource, but such monopolistic exploitation is not at issue here.

the present issue which is to make the best use of the roads we have at any particular point of time. It should by now be obvious that gasoline taxes paid in respect of a vehicle, being only very loosely related to its utilization in congested conditions, do relatively little to optimize road usage. What is needed are charges for road use which are closely related to the amount of use made of congested roads at times of congestion. Modern technology has made possible several ways of achieving this.[12]

A tax may also be the best method of dealing with unidirectional external diseconomies when the numbers of people or firms concerned is so large that only collective action is possible. On the other hand, it may not be the best method. Writers of economic textbooks like to use the example of smoke nuisance, but none has explained how a smoke tax could in practice be levied or has discussed how its rate should vary with the height of the chimney or the composition of the smoke, though both are relevant to the amount of damage caused.

Finally, we come back to the point that fairness matters, too, and may even justify a tax which has no effects on resource allocation. Thus consider the following extract from a statement made by the Minister of Aviation in the House of Commons on March 10, 1965:

> After reviewing the measures currently being taken, we have come to the conclusion that some further assistance should be offered to residents in the vicinity of Heathrow. The volume of traffic, particularly jet traffic, at Heathrow is far greater than at any other aerodrome in this country and is bound to increase. We have, therefore, decided to accept the principle of the recommendation, made in the report of Sir Alan Wilson's Committee on Noise, about the soundproofing of rooms in private dwellings.
>
> Grants of 50 per cent subject to a maximum of £100, of the cost of soundproofing up to three rooms will be made available to householders in a defined area round Heathrow for work carried out with prior approval and to an approved design. The work must be completed by 31st December, 1970, when the scheme will come to an end. These grants will be payable in respect of soundproofing of existing private dwellings and those completed by 1st January, 1966, and will be confined to owners or residents in the defined areas on that date.
>
> The Government consider that the cost of these grants should fall on those whose activities cause the disturbance, or those who benefit from such activities. We intend, therefore, to introduce an Amendment to the Airports Authority Bill at present before Parliament to enable these grants to be paid by the British Airports Authority under a detailed scheme which will be published by Statutory Instrument. It will be for the Authority to determine whether, and, if so, how, their revenues need to be increased to

---

[12] The subject has been splendidly investigated by a panel set up by the Minister of Transport. Its report *Road Pricing: The Economic and Technical Possibilities* was published by Her Majesty's Stationery Office in 1964.

meet the cost of these grants. Local authorities around Heathrow will be asked to help the Airports Authority in administering the scheme.

The "tax" to be paid by the Airports Authority does not increase with the amount of noise, so is not a tax designed to discourage noise. Its purpose is purely to serve equity, and noise is controlled by the imposition of noise level limits on jets using the airport.

Regulation, contracts (or legal actions) and taxes are thus three ways of dealing with external economies and diseconomies. A fourth way, which deserves mention for the sake of completeness, is what economists call "internalizing the externalities." The problem to be faced is that of causing one or more separate decision-making units to take account of the impact of their activities upon other such units. Centralizing decision making for the group of units could clearly achieve this result. Thus, if a particular fishery were exploited by a single concern rather than by a number of separate fishermen, it could take into account the interaction between the activities of the fishermen acting under its control. This serves to show what is meant by "internalizing" and that is all that is necessary here.

This completes our review. The main points which I have made are that each case must be considered on its merits and that these should be set out in economic terms as far as possible. Administrators should consider alternatives to direct regulation, economists should not exaggerate the applicability of tax devices, and both should remember that, in a democratic country, questions of fairness require legal or political decisions.

Roland N. McKean

SOME PROBLEMS OF CRITERIA AND ACQUIRING INFORMATION

I have almost no adverse criticisms of Mr. Turvey's paper. My discussion will only re-emphasize some of the many good features and indicate a few supplementary points and slight changes in emphasis that may be worth consideration.

One excellent feature is his stress on the idea that action concerning an externality is appropriate only if the gains promise to exceed the costs. That is, the existence of a side effect does not automatically mean that a better situation is attainable, and only rarely would complete elimination of an existing side effect be economical. To eliminate an external cost completely would be much like producing any commodity to the point where the marginal value would be zero, and this is rarely appropriate, because at that point one is surely sacrificing other outputs that have more value than this output.

In general, one should take action only if the gains promise to exceed the costs, whatever his value system. If he approves the value system that is implicit in our private market economy or in our mixed economy, then he will approve measuring those gains and costs in market prices. If he has some other value system, if, for example, he attaches great weight to the well-being of posterity, he may prefer to measure gains and losses in a somewhat different way, but the general principle will, of course, still be true.

Roland N. McKean *is professor of economics at the University of California, Los Angeles. From 1951 to 1963, with the exception of a year at the University of Glasgow as a Fulbright scholar, he was a research economist with the RAND Corporation. His books include* Efficiency in Government Through Systems Analysis, Economics of Defense in the Nuclear Age *(co-author with Charles Hitch), and (with Joseph A. Kershaw)* Teacher Shortages and Salary Schedules. *He is also author of numerous journal articles and chapters of books. Mr. McKean was born in Milberry Grove, Illinois, in 1917, and received his A.B. and Ph.D. degrees in economics from the University of Chicago.*

It is not surprising that Mr. Turvey should stress this point; he has shown keen awareness of it in his previous work. But it is a proposition that is worth considerable emphasis, because there has been a tendency to neglect it—to feel that if there is an external cost it should be abolished. The presence of an externality is a departure from the ideal in the same sense that limited resources and harsh winters are departures from the ideal; but these phenomena are not necessarily departures from attainable "optimality."

In addition, Mr. Turvey stresses the fact that judgments upon fairness properly enter into decisions about the actions to be taken by government. Along this same line, he might also have reminded readers that judgments upon other things may also legitimately enter into these choices, for there is no ultimate criterion of correctness in group decision making. If there is not unanimity, individuals may well agree on some rule rather than fight, but there is still no fundamentally correct criterion.

Because of equity considerations, one may prefer one point to another, or he may prefer a point inside the efficiency boundary to many points that are on the boundary. (Indeed, one may prefer some position to *any* point that someone else *says* is on the boundary, for he may disbelieve that the alleged boundary is really attainable.) In addition, however, there can be legitimate disagreement about the nature of the boundary, because there can be disagreement about the prices that should be attached to various effects (i.e., goods and services). This is true of both side effects and effects that are bought and sold in markets.

Thus government officials, like anyone else, can believe that market valuations are inappropriate—e.g., that the price of steel mills ought to be higher relative to that of night clubs because the former investment contributes more to long-run growth or the latter investment is regarded as immoral. Individuals can also disagree about the value tags that should be attached to side effects. For example, some persons could believe that noise and smog are good for people because they stiffen the moral fiber of mankind. As Joseph Schumpeter once mentioned, a person may prefer socialist bread (or capitalist bread) even if it has mice in it. All this is merely to say: It is not necessarily illogical for many considerations other than fairness to influence one's views on policies regarding externalities. Let us put these considerations aside, however, and focus our attention on efficiency in the usual sense— inability to make one person better off (as *he* sees it) without making someone else worse off (as *he* sees it).

To repeat, Mr. Turvey points out that action is called for only if it appears that the gains would exceed the costs. One may get a bit more insight into the matter if he thinks about this in terms of the cost of acquiring the relevant information. In this connection, I shall draw partly on Turvey's own work but especially on the work of Harold Demsetz.[1] The basic difficulty in deciding what to do about externalities is the cost of learning about the costs and gains from alternative courses of action. One way of simultaneously getting information and coping with a side effect is to define individual property rights clearly and set up a market for the external effect. Drivers of sports cars, for example, might have to buy householders' permission to inject noise into their respective sound-spaces, or householders might have to pay the drivers to get mufflers or cease driving noisy vehicles. Bids for and offers of noise reduction can be visualized, information about individuals' subjective values of incremental noise abatement would be generated, and whatever quantity of the product was worth its cost would be produced.

Needless to say, however, this method of getting the information and internalizing the externality would be terribly expensive. Indeed the reason noise production is an externality in the first place is that transaction costs are so high. Usually (though not always) the externality is a public good or bad, and one particular element of transaction costs— the cost of erecting barriers to exclude non-payers so that a price of admission could be charged—is extremely large. In some instances other elements of transaction costs, that is, the costs of operating markets, are quite high too. As an example involving both exclusion costs and other transaction costs, consider the reduction of noise inflicted on people by sports cars. The costs of defining rights to sound-space, excluding those who would not pay for noise abatement (or for rights to invade sound-spaces), arranging contracts between thousands of householders and thousands of sports-car drivers, and enforcing the contracts would be enormous. It may be that government action can sometimes facilitate such transactions and reduce their costs. In the main, however, our concern is with side effects in situations where government can do little to make markets for those effects economical.

One turns, therefore, to other ways of acquiring information about the costs and gains of alternative steps intended to improve the situation. Unfortunately, these other methods of getting information of similar quality turn out to be extremely expensive too. Consider estimating the value of incremental noise abatement (or of any other nonmarketed product, such as better schools or parks for other people's children).

---

[1] I have benefited from past discussions with Demsetz, and also Armen Alchian, and am particularly indebted to Demsetz for access to his "The Exchange and Enforcement of Property Rights," *Journal of Law and Economics,* October 1964, pp. 11–26, and his "Private Property, Information, and Efficiency" (unpublished paper).

Most persons would attach positive value to these items, but, as has long been recognized, one cannot obtain reliable information by asking individuals how much they would voluntarily pay to have specified increments. Nor can one sort out dependable information by examining the prices paid for substitutes, such as the values sacrificed in order to move to quieter locations. What *is* the quantity of noise abatement that is being purchased? How much *is* being paid for the noise reduction, since the sacrifice entailed by moving is seldom clear and the action may purchase other benefits as well? And without markets is there any reason to believe that a few persons' implied evaluations have *any relationship* to the marginal evaluations of other persons? It is very difficult to determine, therefore, whether urban noise is becoming a major source of distress or merely a minor nuisance that is interesting to talk about but is not worth much sacrifice to avoid. Information as good as that generated by markets is impossible to get—that is, it is infinitely expensive. In cost-benefit analyses, we properly settle for lower-quality information but must constantly ask whether the information is worth its cost. Also we must keep the quality of the information in mind when asking which step, if any, to regulate an externality is worth its cost.

Another aspect of side effects that, in my view, deserves more emphasis (and study) is the fact that they are pervasive within the government sector. Mr. Turvey's definition still applies: Side effects are impacts that "are exerted otherwise than through the market." If a government official's decision uses only inputs that are purchased or obtained with the voluntary consent of an owner and yields outputs that are disposed of through voluntary exchange, the impacts are internalized and there are no side effects. Needless to say, government agencies often make use of resources that have value to other agencies or individuals without buying voluntary consent, and they dispense to other agencies or individuals benefits that are not sold. (Thus the recipients' valuations cannot be observed.) The bargaining mechanism works to internalize part of the gains and costs inflicted on others but in an exceedingly imprecise fashion.

The situation is quite similar to the examples pertaining to the private sector. The rights of individual officials and nongovernment personnel to certain resources and their services are ill defined, and in effect the governmental decision makers have no right to capture certain gains they produce, and they do have rights to avoid part of the costs they cause. Even if all rights could be neatly defined and assigned, the costs of excluding nonpayers from using resources and the costs of making and enforcing innumerable contracts would be extremely high. Inside the public sector itself, then, we introduce regulations and constraints on various parts of government in an effort to cope with side effects. Here too we grope for those regulations, bargaining arrangements, and rules of thumb that appear to yield more gain than cost; though often we make mistakes.

Even government regulations intended to cope with externalities produce in turn their own side effects. A blanket prohibition of cesspools to reduce spillovers into a community's underground water supply would not only prohibit actions that in some circumstances would be economic but might also lead districts to conduct effluents to some body of water where it would pollute another community's supply. Federal setting of health and education standards for local communities might produce a subtle side effect—the erosion of local autonomy—which, though it might be of great importance, would be extremely hard to evaluate. While we know that many persons would be willing to pay something to prevent increments in such erosion, it would be difficult to determine how much. There is nothing inherently wrong, of course, with the creation of some externalities in order to alleviate difficulties caused by others. (It may take one to catch one, so to speak.)

In conclusion, I might mention a couple of minor quibbles. In Mr. Turvey's discussion of the levying of a tax or charge on the use of a common property resource, it might be mentioned again that this would be appropriate only if the gains were believed to exceed the transaction and policing costs of doing so. To say this to Mr. Turvey is carrying coals to Newcastle, but for many of his readers this general point may be worth frequent mention. A little later on he says that "urban roads differ from the other two examples [the fish stock and the underground water supply] in that the amount available is entirely within the control of man." As I see it, the difference is merely one of degree; man can, if he chooses, restock even ocean fisheries and recharge underground water supplies. But these two remarks show mainly the desperate lengths to which I am driven in order to produce any unfavorable comments on Mr. Turvey's paper.

Chapter Four

ECONOMIC RESEARCH IN PROBLEMS OF ENVIRONMENT

Allen V. Kneese

⟨ RESEARCH GOALS AND ⟩
⟨ PROGRESS TOWARD THEM ⟩

Useful study of environmental quality problems requires a wide understanding of the physical and social worlds and their interrelationships. As man's ability to work vast changes on particular aspects of his environment becomes greater and people are more and more strongly and directly affected by the activities of others, the need for comprehensive understanding becomes more critical. But striving for broad understanding is no substitute for immediate efforts to illuminate particular aspects of the problem. Such clarification is perhaps most urgently needed in the social and biological sciences. My main object is to report on research in one of these areas—economics.

Economic studies of environmental quality have a short history and perhaps it is too early for a formal assessment. Nevertheless, I think there are enough results to support some opinions on the direction and scope of work done so far, on strong points and gaps in current research, and on the bearing these efforts have on appropriate public policy and techniques of planning toward optimum environmental quality.

In commenting on some of the important economic studies which are completed or in progress, I shall divide them into four categories: (a) conceptual and methodological studies; (b) empirical evaluation studies; (c) studies of control systems; and (d) studies bearing upon desirable institutional change. Most of the examples I shall cite are either under-

Allen V. Kneese *is director of RFF's research programs in water resources and in quality of the environment. Previous to joining RFF he was research associate with the Federal Reserve Bank of Kansas City and before that assistant professor of economics at the University of New Mexico. Among his books are* Water Pollution: Economic Aspects and Research Needs *and* The Economics of Regional Water Quality Management. *He is also author of numerous journal articles in his fields, and is co-editor of the quarterly journal* Water Resources Research. *Mr. Kneese was born in 1930 in Fredericksburg, Texas. He received his B.S. from Southwest Texas College and his Ph.D. in economics from the University of Indiana.*

69

taken or sponsored by Resources for the Future. One reason for this is that these are the enterprises with which I am most familiar; but the main reason, I believe, is that this is an area in which RFF is concentrating much effort.

A comparatively detailed conceptual study[1] of water pollution has been published; a similar study of pesticides by J. C. Headley and J. N. Lewis has been completed with RFF support and is being prepared for publication. Some work of this kind concerning air has been completed[2] and an intensive study is now under way.[3] A current RFF staff effort seeks to provide a framework of concepts and research methodologies for such problems of the rural and back country environment, as curtailing landscape deterioration and providing for optimum wildlife production. In general, these studies take off from the framework of thought known as welfare economics—though all recognize that its concepts and theories must be interpreted flexibly and adapted to the facts of particular cases.

The benefit-cost analysis used in conjunction with water resources project planning and evaluation can be thought of as the most advanced field of *applied* welfare economics. But, despite some substantial practical successes and the efforts of various writers to clarify the matter, the application of economic theory to problems of public policy is still widely misunderstood.

There is still a tendency to think of "economic" as being narrowly concerned with financial returns. Actually, welfare economics endeavors systematically to incorporate values which are not registered in market prices, although where possible "willingness to pay" is used as a surrogate measure. It is often feasible to impute such a measure from market evidence, with the aid of some assumptions about human behavior. For example, one can try to measure the economic value of aesthetic responses to air pollution by observing the influence which air pollution has on property values.

To my knowledge, the scope of welfare economics has never been described better than in the following statement by Mason Gaffney:

[1] Allen V. Kneese, *Water Pollution: Economic Aspects and Research Needs* (Washington: Resources for the Future, Inc., 1961).

[2] See M. Mason Gaffney, "Applying Economic Controls," and Thomas D. Crocker, "In Polk and Hillsborough Counties, Florida," in *Bulletin of the Atomic Scientists*, June 1965. See also the papers in Harold Wolozin (ed.), *The Economics of Air Pollution* (New York: W. W. Norton, 1966).

[3] Under the direction of Professor Robert Strotz with the support of an RFF grant to Northwestern University.

One of the most important functions of economic analysis is to evaluate public policy. Economics, contrary to common usage, begins with the postulate that man is the measure of all things. Direct damage to human health and happiness is more directly "economic," therefore, than damage to property which is simply an intermediate means to health and happiness. Neither do economists regard "economic" as a synonym for "pecuniary." Rather money is but one of many means to ends, as well as a useful measure of value. "Economic damage" therefore includes damages to human function and pleasure. The economist tries to weigh these direct effects on people in the same balance with other costs and benefits—to the end of making decisions to maximize net social benefits . . . [when this is done] one can decide which of many options is best, securing maximum net benefits over costs. And, having so decided, one can devise means to compensate the losers from the gains of the winners in the interests of distributive equity.[4]

Management of environmental quality, as the welfare economist understands it, has two aspects.

The first reflects the external effects which Ralph Turvey has described in the preceding chapter. The idea of balancing internal costs of control against the external costs imposed is persuasive, has a certain amount of legal sanction ("balancing equities" can be interpreted this way), and can in theory be carried out with great mathematical precision. Some economists in developing this concept have used the infinitesimal calculus to indicate the condition for optimality, i.e., the situation which must prevail if the net benefits from control are to be at a maximum.

However, continued statements that water should be as clean as physically possible, that the air must never be used for waste disposal, and that no bird or beast should ever be the victim of a pesticide, forcefully show that even the elementary idea of measuring costs against benefits has not penetrated very far. The cost of achieving such ideals could be tremendous. For water alone, a rough calculation indicates that to return all effluents to water courses in a state equal to pristine purity might cost $20 billion a year—about as much as we spend for primary and secondary education. I am sure that most people would find such an undertaking ridiculous. At the other extreme, unmitigated discharge to water courses of raw domestic sewage, slaughterhouse offal, sulfuric acid, and other equally distressing substances would surely have important property damage and direct human welfare costs. Similar points could be made in regard to the other environmental quality impacts with which we are concerned.

[4] M. Mason Gaffney, "Applying Economic Controls," *Bulletin of the Atomic Scientists,* June 1965, p. 20.

What is the proper balance? Economic concepts suggest an answer but the necessary measurements are often exceedingly difficult to perform. However, there has been some progress which I will return to shortly. But once the proper balance has been decided on, how can it be attained? As Mr. Turvey points out, there is a considerable difference of opinion between economists and administrators. The latter tend to favor standards and rules governing specific types of behavior. The former tend to prefer price-like devices such as taxes or effluent charges. The point usually, but not always properly,[5] turns on issues of administrative feasibility and equity. The administrators have usually won, but evidence that the economists' viewpoint is making headway is found in the mounting discussion within the federal government on effluent charges or taxes as a way of controlling water quality.

The second aspect of the economics of environmental management is more like the established application of benefit-cost analysis to public investment in water development, transport, and so on. In most, if not all, fields of environmental management there are potentially effective and efficient measures which cannot be achieved by setting standards or even imposing taxes upon the behavior of individual decision makers who cause externalities (or spillover). One way of putting this is that inhering in certain devices are economies of scale which cannot be realized by the individual, firm, or even the individual community.

Within the environmental quality field the most intensively analyzed of these "regional-scale opportunities" are in water quality management. These include reservoirs for flow regulation to increase waste dilution and a variety of means to improve or make better use of the assimilative capacity of streams. Conceptual studies have recognized and described these options and indeed some scholars have worked out rather detailed criteria for decisions with respect to them. But the problem becomes an exceedingly complex one which involves incorporating optimum behavior rules or incentives in a system which also includes regional scale measures. These considerations have led economists to use techniques of operation research or system analysis suitable for the organization and manipulation of data relating to complex systems exhibiting myriads of interdependencies. Institutional changes that might improve the design, implementation, and operation of such systems also have been discussed, although largely at the conceptual level. Most, if not all, economists who have looked at problems of environmental quality con-

[5] Allen V. Kneese, *The Economics of Regional Water Quality Management* (Baltimore: The Johns Hopkins Press for Resources for the Future, Inc., 1964), pp. 83–84.

ceptually would agree that it is improbable that optimal systems could be obtained simply by the imposition of rules and incentives on the individuals, firms, and communities responsible for environmental impacts.

Evaluation studies are concerned largely with (1) the willingness of individual decision units (municipalities, industries, and individuals—ultimately always individuals) to pay for the avoidance of damages, and (2) what the cost would be to those decision units that found it necessary to take mitigating action to reduce external costs.

Damage Costs. Again the greatest progress has been made in the area of water pollution. Several industry studies by RFF staff members or grantees are at various stages. Among other things, they seek to assess the net damage which industries suffer when they have to use low quality water. Since a variety of adjustments are possible, the problem becomes complex. Several studies have been models of ingenuity in using limited data and modeling or simulating effects on industrial processes. Some preliminary results are available for the pulp and paper, petroleum refining, canning, thermal power and sugar beet industries, although none of these studies is finished. In all of them industrial costs appear to be surprisingly insensitive to water quality within comparatively wide ranges —especially in regard to aspects of quality that are usually influenced by prior uses and discharge of effluents. Sensitivity is greater to pollutants that in most cases are of natural origin, such as chlorides and magnesium. One important reason for the comparative insensitivity is that the vast proportion of industrial water use is for purposes that can readily accommodate low quality—cooling for instance. A second reason is that the really sensitive processes—like those involving high pressure boilers—ordinarily need water of such high quality that extensive treatment is necessary if *any* kind of river water is used; water of distinctly low quality can be used with only minor incremental costs. High pressure boiler feed water must be distilled and the cost of distillation is not particularly sensitive to the quality of intake water. The moral of this is that not much pollution control can be justified by benefits to industrial users.

The situation is surprisingly similar for municipal water supplies. Much of what has been said about the need for high quality water supplies as a basis for preparation of potable water seems more the product of emotion than of logic. The water of the much discussed Hudson River, which many believe should not be used for municipal supply because of its poor quality, is actually about like that at the Torresdale intake of the city of Philadelphia. This water has for many years, through use of very well understood technology, been prepared for acceptable drinking water—albeit at the expense of some extra chemical applications. Moreover, a water treatment plant at Dusseldorf, Germany, using activated carbon and ozone, makes perfectly acceptable drinking water from the Rhine which is in far worse shape than either the Delaware or the Hudson. Poor water quality does impose extra costs for municipal water treatment but—except in cases of extremely toxic or evil-tasting substances—it ordinarily cannot justify very high levels of waste effluent treatment.

This point is brought out in a recent study of a stream system along whose shores are municipal waste dischargers and municipal water users. The study involved a very careful gathering of cost data and even the generation of new cost information. It also developed a sophisticated technique for tracing by means of computer simulation the interrelationship between water quality at waste outfalls and at water intakes. The study concluded that vast amounts of reuse are required to justify the additional costs of advanced sewage treatment for municipal waste disposal.[6] For example, the study indicated that water withdrawal for municipal water treatment downstream required to justify additional upstream sewage treatment costs solely on savings to downstream water treatment plants is on the order of 16 to 250 to 1 for small sewage treatment plants and 10 to 30 to 1 for large sewage treatment plants. Again it appears that the need to prepare drinking water cannot justify particularly high standards of stream water quality.

But to go back to Mr. Gaffney's statement quoted earlier, direct effects on people's satisfactions are the most straightforwardly "economic" of all and it is in them that we must seek the major justification for high water quality in streams—if indeed such a justification exists.

There is, of course, clear evidence of a close relationship between water quality and human satisfactions. It does not seem to arise from a feeling that health is really endangered to any great extent, or that the cost of manufactured goods has been substantially increased because manufacturers have had to provide costly treatment to the water they use. Rather, it is seen in the reactions of the fisherman who has experienced aesthetically displeasing water (perhaps with dead fish in it) and of the person who just prefers to see a clear stream and might even be willing to sacrifice something else (pay higher local taxes? or pay higher prices for manufactured goods?) to get it. Politicians have been sensitive

[6] Richard J. Frankel, "Water Quality Management: Engineering-Economic Factors in Municipal Waste Disposal," *Water Resources Research*, Vol. 1, No. 2 (2nd Quarter, 1965).

to these feelings which have permitted, if not induced, progressively stronger federal legislation in recent years.

But politically expressed discontent is a highly generalized phenomenon. It does not say much about whether action is justified in a particular instance and, if so, how much. What standard for a body of water will balance costs and gains in a particular instance? Clearly it depends on circumstances. How much does it cost to improve quality? What present and future uses does the water have? What alternatives are there? Economic analysis can go some distance in helping to answer all these questions.

Meanwhile, how important are the values that persons might attach to water quality for recreation purposes? As I have already noted, decisions concerning water quality must often, if not usually, turn upon this kind of value. A useful study of the recreational value of water quality is under way in the Delaware estuary on whose shores there is perhaps the greatest urban-industrial complex in the United States. The estuary experiences low—even zero—dissolved oxygen almost every year during low-flow periods. To raise D.O. is an expensive proposition. It would cost about $100 million of investment to raise it to two parts per million and around $300 million to raise it to four parts per million.[7] Gigantic as these costs are, an econometric study of potential increases in participation rates shows that these higher oxygen levels might be justified on recreational grounds alone. These preliminary results suggest that placing a value on increased boating of about $2.50 a day might justify maintaining three parts per million of D.O. even if no other benefits were considered.[8] At today's levels of discretionary income, $2.50 a day does not seem to be an extravagant value to attach to a day of boating. We badly need more and better studies of this kind if our water quality objectives are to have any rational basis. In some instances it might be found that where good alternative recreation opportunities are available, and high quality water in a particular stream is expensive to attain, it might be best to use that stream heavily for waste disposal.

While dependable and systematic damage information with respect to water pollution is still quite thin, we are even worse off in regard to other aspects of environmental quality. Extraordinarily interesting and

[7] Department of Health, Education, and Welfare, "Federal Water Pollution Control Administration, Delaware Estuary Comprehensive Study—Report on Alternative Water Quality Improvement Programs," February 1966, p. 10.

[8] Paul Davidson, F. Gerard Adams, and Joseph Seneca, "The Social Value of Water Recreational Facilities Resulting from an Improvement in Water Quality: The Delaware Estuary," in Allen V. Kneese and Stephen C. Smith (eds.), *Water Research* (Baltimore: The Johns Hopkins Press for Resources for the Future, Inc., 1966).

potentially useful work is, however, progressing in regard to air pollution.[9] Several strategies for measuring the impacts of air pollution have
been tried experimentally. The most interesting is measurement of air
pollution impacts upon property values. Property values can be a surrogate for all the various direct and indirect impacts of an adverse
environmental change. This has been explained as follows: ". . . so far
as air pollution is concerned, there is one market that is more likely
than others to reflect the majority of effects. This is the land, or real
estate, market. If the land market were to work perfectly, the price of
a plot of land would equal the sum of the present discounted stream
of benefits and costs derivable from it. If some of its costs rise (e.g.,
additional maintenance and cleaning costs are required) or some of its
benefits fall (e.g., one cannot see the mountains from the terrace) the
property will be discounted in the market to reflect people's evaluation
of these changes. Since air pollution is specific to locations and the
supply of locations is fixed, there is less likelihood that the negative
effects of pollution can be significantly shifted onto other markets. We
should therefore, expect to find the majority of effects reflected in this
market, and can measure them by observing associated changes in
property value."[10]

This idea sounds simple; putting it to use is far from simple. Great
statistical ingenuity is needed to isolate from all other determinants the
effect of one of the elements—air pollution—that bear upon property
values. Nevertheless, analysis has now made clear that impacts on land
values and therefore upon all the human values which attach to particular sites can be substantial. A study in St. Louis found that property
values are linearly related to mean annual sulfation rates. When sulfation
levels were divided into eight equal zones of rising intensity, values ap-
peared to decline about $250.00 per lot, per zone, other things remaining
constant.[11] This would appear to be enough to justify even a costly
control effort but it also seems that the disbenefit that people attach to
air pollution is finite and possibly fairly measurable. It does not suggest
that total prohibitions on use of the air's assimilative capacity is usually
the right answer. The problem, rather, is one of determining costs and
gains.

Environmental deterioration may affect human health, in the strict
sense of the word, as well as welfare. Estimates of the economic impacts

[9] See Ronald Ridker, *Economic Costs of Air Pollution, Studies in Measurement*
(New York: Frederick A. Praeger, Inc., 1966); and Crocker, *op. cit.*
[10] Ronald Ridker, "Strategies for Measuring the Cost of Air Pollution," in
Wolozin, *op. cit.*, pp. 87–101.
[11] *Ibid.*

of a number of diseases have been made,[12] and there is now considerable literature discussing the pros and cons of particular methods of measurement. Agreement seems to be developing that the most useful measure so far devised is the present or capitalized value of the gross production lost. No economist presents these measures as a full evaluation of the costs—including the psychic costs—of illness and death and they are perhaps more useful for comparative purposes than for measuring absolute values.

Even the absolute measures may be of some utility, however, in that they can indicate the minimal cost which society can attach to disease and this may suggest whether expenditures for research and control are far out of line. It is clear that the cost of even some of the less virulent diseases is very high. For example, the following total costs have been computed for diseases which may be associated with air pollution.[13]

Cancer of the respiratory system	$680.0 million
Chronic bronchitis	159.7 "
Acute bronchitis	6.2 "
Common cold	331.0 "
Pneumonia	490.0 "
Emphysema	64.0 "
Asthma	259.0 "
	$1,989.9 million

This sums up to a truly impressive loss—but of course far from all of this is attributable to air pollution. If we wished to use economic loss calculations in a systematic way for decision making, we would need to know not only what portion of existing disease costs is due to air pollution but also how the various categories of cost vary with changes in concentrations and lengths of exposure. This is an area in which the capacity of medical science to forecast physiological effects falls short even of our ability to predict economic impacts. I know of no medical scientist willing to define any quantitative relationship between the unwanted ingestion or inhalation of chemical and biological residuals at

[12] See Burton A. Weisbrod, *Economics of Public Health* (Philadelphia: University of Pennsylvania Press, 1961); Herbert E. Klarman, "Syphilis Control Programs," in Robert Dorfman (ed.), *Measuring the Benefits of Government Investments* (Washington: The Brookings Institution, 1965); Ronald Ridker, "Economic Costs of Air Pollution," *op. cit.* The Klarman paper contains useful references to additional works on the economics of health.

[13] Ridker, *Economic Costs of Air Pollution, Studies in Measurement, op. cit.* These include four categories of cost—those due to premature death, morbidity, treatment, and prevention. They are capitalized for the year 1958 at a 5 per cent interest rate.

levels existing in our current environment and the rates and intensities of disease. Until this is possible, economic and other research that could assist decision making with respect to health impacts will be stymied.

Let me make so bold as to express some qualitative judgments on strictly health losses in the United States due to environmental impacts considered in this paper.

Character of Environmental Impact	Physical Effect	Economic Loss
Water pollution	No discernible effect except in isolated instances where it is usually due to malfunction of equipment.	Probably minor
Pesticide residual	No evidence of any effect except occasionally to those involved directly in manufacture and use.	Probably minor
Air pollution	Statistical correlations exist relating incidence of certain respiratory diseases to air pollution levels —several catastrophes have occurred in recent years.	Probably substantial

The health effects of air and water pollution differ principally because surface water is seldom ingested in an untreated state while air almost always is. The current disease-causing potential of raw water is actually much higher than that of raw air but we are able to exercise control over it at points of emission *and* before ingestion—the latter usually being much more effective. I have elsewhere remarked that with respect to air pollution we are somewhat in the same position as the fish are in regard to water pollution—we live in it.

Control Costs. The costs of controlling unfavorable impacts on the environment are no less important than the costs of damage, but in some ways the problems they present are simpler. This doesn't mean they are easily solved; furthermore, in many cases where measurement would seem to be rather straightforward, remarkably little has actually been performed.

For instance, the RFF industry studies mentioned earlier endeavor to determine what the optimal adjustments to various levels of effluent control would be and how much they would cost. Despite the fact that this is absolutely basic information for any rational control policy, these few studies appear to be the only ones which generate such information in a systematic way. However, tentative as their results are at present, they teach some important lessons which appear to be confirmed by scattered information from other industries as well.

Industrial waste loads create large problems. The U.S. Public Health Service estimates that about twice as much organic waste is discharged by industry as by all municipalities combined and that industry discharges an even larger proportion of other wastes.[14] I have calculated that if the beet sugar industry were to continue to discharge organic waste at the mid-century rate per unit of output, the load coming from this one small part of the food industry by the year 2000 would be equal to about half of that discharged today by all municipalities in the United States combined.[15]

Two closely related and important conclusions are emerging from the economic studies of industrial waste disposal. One is that currently existing plants generate (i.e., produce before any final effluent treatment) vastly different amounts of waste. In the sugar beet industry this ranges from wastes equivalent to those from a city of one-half million persons to zero. The other is that the costs associated with waste control differ greatly from plant to plant. There are several reasons for this— among them are the age and basic design of the plant, the market conditions for recovered materials, and the particular types of raw materials and fuels used.

All this suggests two important policy implications:

(a) An effluent standard that is uniform from plant to plant would impose much higher per unit costs of control on some plants than others. This means that shifting control from one plant to another could reduce, perhaps greatly, the private and social cost of achieving a particular level of stream water quality. The effluent charge or tax often advocated by economists tends to concentrate waste reduction at those locations where it can be accomplished least expensively.

(b) Subsidization of waste water treatment equipment, which has frequently been proposed in the Congress and in state legislatures, would bias the technique used for control in an uneconomical direction. It would tend to promote construction of treatment facilities even though adjustments in processes, products, or inputs can achieve the same result at less cost. Again a technique, such as the effluent charge, which allows

[14] See Murray Stein, "Problems and Programs in Water Pollution," *Natural Resources Journal* (December 1962), pp. 397–98.

[15] Based on a projection of sugar demand, found on pages 249 and 250 of Hans H. Landsberg, Leonard L. Fischman, and Joseph L. Fisher, *Resources in America's Future* (Baltimore: The Johns Hopkins Press for Resources for the Future, Inc., 1963).

individual optimizing adjustments would produce the more efficient result.

Individually tailored standards could in principle achieve the same effect. But this would require detailed knowledge of industrial processes, costs, and probable future technological opportunities which research might produce—a level of knowledge well beyond that which regulating authorities now have or perhaps can ever be expected to have. The argument for putting an explicit price on the use of the waste-assimilative and transport capacities of water courses and permitting individual waste dischargers to adjust to it is most compelling with respect to industry but is applicable to municipalities too.

Considerable work has been done on the costs of municipal waste treatment and even some projections of technology have been attempted.[16] In general, research has shown that any desired degree of reduction of impurities in municipal waste streams can be achieved although costs rise very rapidly when 100 per cent removal is approached. For example, costs about double when removal of Biochemical Oxygen Demand from a municipal effluent increases from 91 or 92 per cent to 96 or 97 per cent. Costs would about triple again should one wish to go from 97 per cent to about 100 per cent. While per capita real costs of municipal sanitation have probably not risen much, if at all, over the past 75 years even though standards of treatment have gradually improved,[17] they could increase sharply should we try to move rapidly toward highly purified effluents—or to put it differently, should we seek to abandon any dependence on the waste assimilative capacity of our surface waters. This might add $10 or $12 billion a year to our national costs just for disposing of household wastes. Thus we must assign high values to in-stream uses if we are rationally to justify standards of water quality which require advanced treatment. Measurement or judgment of values in this connection is no small undertaking, but one that cannot be avoided.

In the course of recent RFF research on the means and costs of water quality control, several unorthodox measures have been evaluated. These include direct introduction of oxygen into water bodies and programmed application of advanced waste treatment techniques during critical periods associated with extreme low flow—both methods are discussed below in connection with the research on waste disposal systems.

In the areas of pesticides, air pollution, and landscape, very little progress has been made on studying the costs of avoiding unfavorable

---

[16] See Frankel, *op. cit.*; and Robert K. Davis, "Planning a Water Quality Management System: The Case of the Potomac Estuary," in Kneese and Smith, *op. cit.*
[17] From an unpublished table prepared by Harold Thomas, Harvard University.

external effects. Some work has been done on the costs of reducing the emission of unburned hydrocarbons from automobiles. It has been suggested, for example, that by the time the required devices are installed on all cars, the cost of automobile exhaust controls in California will be several hundred million and may be as high as a billion dollars. Even so, it is questionable whether these controls are adequate for the future. It has been estimated that in Los Angeles, if the pattern of automobile use continues, the area's population continues to grow at its present rate, and present control standards are unchanged, the automobile pollution problem will be as bad in a decade as it is now.[18] Once again, this illustrates that high levels of control imply a major commitment of resources—certainly tens of billions of dollars for automobile controls alone at the national level. As must be clear by now, I am not implying that such a level of expenditure is improper or that even higher levels of control might not be justified. But it is equally clear that the stakes involved do invite a major effort to understand what will be the best levels and means of control.

As in the case of water pollution, there may be some administrative and regulatory alternatives to standards for air pollution control that demand serious consideration. One example is some variety of air pollution charge or tax. This would be levied on the theory that use of a congested facility, air, should be reduced by putting a price on its use. In principle, such a tax should be based on some measure of pollutant discharged at the source and could be weighted according to location of the source, the external costs of specific pollutants, timing of releases in relation to peak loads of air congestion, wind direction, etc. But this approach needs looking into from the point of view of administrative costs and this is where studies of the economics of control can be helpful.

It may be sometimes more feasible and economical to alter the character of some manufactured input, the use of which results in pollution, than to deal with the immediate source of pollution itself. This suggests that taxation or other means of regulation of particular manufactured products which themselves ultimately become pollutants may be useful and effective. To draw an example from water programs, it would not have been feasible to charge or regulate each commercial and household user of "hard" water-polluting detergents, and treating them in sewage treatment plants would have been very costly, but it was feasible to put pressure upon manufacturers to produce bio-degradable types. Indeed

[18] John R. Goldsmith, "Urban Air Conservation," *Bulletin of the Atomic Scientists,* November 1961.

an explicit economic study of the alternative of treating detergents in the plants of the Ruhr River associations quantified the cost of this alternative and led to the German law forbidding the sale of hard detergents.[19]

Along similar lines, it appears that desulfurization of residual fuel oil at the refinery may cost about the same as scrubbing stack gas at utility plants themselves for the removal of sulfur dioxide.[20] Desulfurization may be the only economically feasible way to remove this major pollutant from certain other emissions, such as those of household heating plants. Various means of controlling the character of fuels need further investigation, including the taxation of those with especially destructive effects—say high sulfur fuel oils. The advantage of the taxation method is that it can achieve a desired degree of control while leaving specific production and consumption decisions decentralized in individual hands. This means that the destructive substance will be automatically eliminated from its least valuable uses—ordinarily by the introduction of substitutes—but will continue in those uses where it is markedly economical. This might well have been a preferable way to deal with hard detergents rather than to forbid their sale outright.

In other areas of environmental quality, studies of the economics of control have hardly gone beyond the stage of hypothesis formation. Let me mention at least briefly a couple of hypotheses with regard to pesticides and the landscape. Preliminary observation by Headley and Lewis has indicated that up to a certain point crop yields respond dramatically to the application of pesticides, but that beyond that point the response is slight—application of greater and greater quantities bring small additions in yield. But because pesticides are very cheap relative to other farm production costs, the farmer tends to use them lavishly. Moreover, because pesticides are cheap, there is little incentive to calculate even direct internal returns with precision. Finally, one may suppose that the amount of pesticide residues having unintended external effects will tend to grow as the rate of application rises. All these things taken together suggest that much of the residue could be controlled at the

[19] Dr. W. Bucksteeg and Dipl.-Ing. v. Möller, "Zur Frage der Beseitigung von Detergentien aus Wasser und Abwasser" (About the Question of Removing Detergents from Water and Wastewater), *Industrieabwässer,* Mai 1961.

[20] Lionel S. Galstaun, Bernard Steigerwald, John H. Ludwig, and Howard R. Garrison, "Economics of Fuel Oil Desulfurization." Presented at the 55th annual meeting of American Institute of Chemical Engineers, Houston, Texas, February 7–11, 1965. The authors report that combustion of petroleum products accounts for more than 22 per cent of all SO_2 emitted in this country. About 85 per cent of the total emission of SO_2 from petroleum products results from combustion of residual fuel oils.

expense of comparatively small sacrifice of crop yield benefit. Economic study focusing upon the net value of output sacrificed, considering the probable low yield response at high levels of application and opportunities to substitute other pest control inputs (like more frequent cultivation) for chemical pesticides should yield quantitative results highly useful for decision making. Research of this kind is now under way. Of course it may also show that should we opt for higher levels of control the cost—in terms of yields—will be high. This would be consistent with earlier conclusions. Efforts to eliminate all pesticide residues—that is, to avoid entirely the use of the dilution capacities of the natural environment—are likely to be high, indeed.

Careful and correctly framed work on the costs of avoiding or controlling external costs can be useful even on such difficult matters as preserving landscapes.

As improvements in transportation and greater demand for minerals make it feasible to extend mining to greater distances from present consumption and transportation centers, areas of great natural beauty may be threatened with disfigurement more frequently than in the past—often by mines whose net contribution to the national product will be almost negligible. In deciding whether the beauty of the area is worth preserving, we must be careful to value correctly the contribution of the mineral deposit to the nation's product. This contribution is not measured by the market value of the ore produced, or by the wages that are paid. The proper measure of what the society sacrifices by not mining the deposit is the surplus returns left over after deducting all expenses from revenues. This profit or rent reflecting the differential quality of the deposit is frequently small even for mines with a large output. In other words, equivalent materials usually could be extracted elsewhere at little additional cost. Thus we may well ask what we would give up if we didn't permit the uranium mining activity which exists on the rim of the Grand Canyon. The answer is probably not much.

The "ubiquitous" mining activities, such as sand and gravel extraction, no doubt have unwelcome side effects in the neighborhood of cities, where they are usually conducted. Yet forbidding them might impose heavy costs. These materials are very heavy and are used in large volume, so that proximity to points of use is important. In this case we may well search for other means of controlling externalities. One such method might be to screen the sites where such activities are carried on.

As in other areas of environmental quality, we can improve our information for making decisions in the social interest if we at least know what must be foregone to achieve an end which certain parts of the society consider desirable. This is true even when we are not able to specifically evaluate the benefit, as indeed we often cannot with regard to the preservation of areas of extraordinary natural beauty, or even of the management of more ordinary landscapes.[21]

Causing the decision maker to take account of the external effects of his individual action is a central tenet of economic policy with respect to environmental quality. In some situations, however, the most efficient course may be to provide collective facilities or take other direct collective action.

There is evidence that if one aims at preserving high levels of dissolved oxygen, it can be less costly to introduce air directly into a river than to require advanced levels of treatment at individual effluent outfalls.[22] Sometimes the construction of reservoirs and release of dilution water during otherwise critical times of water pollution will be less costly than more local measures for dealing with the problem. Large-scale biological control of the blowfly has been achieved at low cost in the South by releasing millions of sterilized males—this substitutes for hundreds of thousands of individual applications of pesticides. Extensive provision and use of mass transportation systems might greatly reduce the air pollution problem in our major cities. "Manufacturing" landscape by the well-planned planting of trees may allow important but conflicting activities be located close to each other but still limit the undesirable external effects.

Rare though economic analysis of these alternatives has been, it has shown that they can be very important. We are, however, usually ill-equipped to evaluate such alternatives and our institutional means for implementing and financing them are even more deficient.

The area in which economic analysis has gone farthest is water pollution. It is also possible to make some tentative suggestions concerning institutional implications of these studies.

Several years ago, I made a study of the Ruhr area of Germany which illustrates the efficacy of a regional approach based upon sound economic principles.[23] The streams which serve the Ruhr region have a very low flow during the summer season—about 400 cubic feet per second. This is only about half of the lowest flow ever recorded on the Potomac River. About 10 million people live in the 50-by-100-mile area.

[21] For a further discussion of the matter addressed in the last few paragraphs, see Orris C. Herfindahl and Allen V. Kneese, *Quality of the Environment* (Washington: Resources for the Future, Inc., 1965), Chapter III.

[22] Davis, *op. cit.*

[23] Allen V. Kneese, "Water Quality Management by Regional Authorities in the Ruhr Area," *Papers and Proceedings of the Regional Science Association,* Vol. 11, 1963.

It is perhaps the world's most heavily industrialized region. Forty per cent of the industrial production of Germany occurs here, including over 80 per cent of the heavy industrial output. The waste disposal demands within this region are immense, yet major sections of the river are so managed that the stream is suitable for recreational purposes including swimming and boating. Moreover, prices of unsubsidized publicly supplied water are as low as, or even lower than, those in any of the other major urban areas of Germany. These results have been attained by co-operative regional management authorities known as *Genossenschaften.*

The following features are central to the success of the system developed by these organizations: First, the engineering system has been specifically designed to meet the needs of the Ruhr region. It is a unique system within Germany. Second, waste disposal is managed on a region-wide basis in which advantage is taken of economies resulting from flow regulation and large-scale treatment and recovery of potential waste products. The regenerative capacity of the streams is utilized to the extent consistent with water quality standards which are based on a variety of water uses in the area. Third, one stream in the region is used in a completely specialized way, being dedicated to waste disposal use only. Fourth, all significant industries and cities in the region pay a charge for the effluent they contribute, based upon periodic tests of the quality and quantity of effluents. This charge is not contingent upon whether the wastes are directly handled in treatment plants or not. In other words, an efficient regional system of works is designed and then charges are distributed in accordance with at least a rough measure of the cost of receiving the specific effluents into the system as a whole. Moreover, municipalities and industrial plants can always reduce their charges by reducing the amount of waste discharged into the system.

This system has produced impressive results. The effluent charge motivates industries to reduce their contribution of waste to rivers. Using the geographic and hydrologic features of the particular river basin in an imaginative and systematic manner to minimize waste disposal costs has undoubtedly reduced costs for the region as a whole. A good illustration of this is the fact that municipalities and industries always have the option of building their own waste treatment plants and thereby reducing the effluent charges levied upon them, but thus far, not a single municipality or industry has chosen to follow this route.

Some of the large gains achieved by a systematic regional approach may be attributable to the density of development in the Ruhr area. Nevertheless, it seems that such an approach could achieve major economies even in less highly developed areas of the United States. For example, my RFF colleague Robert Davis has made a case study of the Potomac Basin in which he considered a number of alternatives including mechanical reaeration, diversion of wastes from critical areas, and periodic programmed introduction of advanced waste treatment at particular treatment plants. He was able to find many combinations of systems less costly than the combination of flow regulation and conventional waste treatment at individual points of waste discharge which had been previously proposed for the basin by the federal planning agencies.[24]

Strong evidence is accumulating to indicate that major economies can be achieved in water quality management by institutions which can give full and flexible consideration to a wide range of alternatives and then implement those that turn out to be best. There is also substantial evidence that the traditional functions of federal, state, and local agencies are not adequate in this regard. The development of the *Genossenschaften* in the Ruhr area, the River Authorities in England, a new law establishing river basin authorities in France, and various developments in the United States are all testimony to the impetus which water quality problems can give to regional (river basin) institutions.

In general, however, the institutional aspects of environmental quality have received far less study than the other aspects of the problem.

This may not be entirely inappropriate because such studies usually are best grounded upon knowledge of available opportunities which can result from reasonably thorough study of the natural science, engineering, and economic aspects of the problem. Only in the area of water quality are we near to having the appropriate groundwork for such studies. But urgent problems are upon us. Indeed, problems are emerging and developing so rapidly that gradual institutional adjustment based on a process of unplanned adaption may be very costly, not only in terms of failure to deal with problems, but in missed opportunities for using efficient measures to do so.

What are the proper institutional arrangements to handle the problems of our air sheds, biological pest controls, systematic production of wildlife and protection of landscape? We know almost nothing about how to design institutions which could systematically search out and implement measures for effective and efficient collective action with respect to these problems. Much less do we know whether institutions should be designed for dealing with the problems individually or in various combinations, or what the best balance is between public or collective authority to directly design and manage facilities on the one hand, and the exercise

[24] Davis, *op. cit.*

of control through charges, taxes, standards and the like on the other. We are largely in the dark concerning the proper geographical scope of such institutions. In some cases, where directly relevant market results are absent and values cannot be imputed from market behavior, we must use political institutions to determine relative preference for various possible outcomes. We need to learn how to design institutions to do this systematically and accurately.

Some research is progressing in these areas, but our understanding is still meager. There are, I think, great opportunities for research and constructive innovations in the areas of politics, law, and administrative organizations based firmly upon knowledge of the technology and economics of alternative systems of management.

Three major conclusions arise from this review of economic studies of environmental quality.

(a) Optimum rules, standards, or other techniques for controlling environmental quality must result from analysis of values, contrary to the usual approach which is still narrowly focused on physical effects and objectives. Research in the economic values associated with environmental management has made significant progress along some lines, but has barely begun to shed light on many difficult problems.

(b) Even carefully determined value-based rules and regulations governing individual, industrial, and local government decisions often cannot achieve optimal environmental quality management; more direct and explicit collective acting on a regional scale is often indicated.

(c) We are ill-equipped institutionally to implement those management systems and procedures which economic and engineering analysis suggests; and appropriate research on how to design suitable institutional and organizational arrangements has hardly begun.

M. Mason Gaffney

WELFARE ECONOMICS AND
THE ENVIRONMENT

It was gracious of Allen Kneese to quote me as an expert on welfare economics. I confess that much of the extensive literature on that subject remains alien to me. I do understand about marginal cost pricing, spillovers, the perils of suboptimizing, and all that. But when the Hamlet School soliloquizes on why we can never decide anything because we can't be sure of everything, and why everything is wrong unless everything else is right, I am quickly sated. That kind of thing would soon render us impotent, unfit to decide or act.

My concept of the proper coverage of welfare economics does coincide with Mr. Kneese's. We share the conviction that it should help with decision, and naturally I applaud his enlightened attitude.

I find much else to applaud in Mr. Kneese's paper, and in the process of saying so I should like to reinforce or illustrate a few points.

I admire his persistence in carrying the gospel of marginal analysis into the alien territory of pollution evaluation and abatement. He seeks to meld theory and practice in a new area, to the mutual gain of practice and theory.

He applies the economists' incremental approach, based on the postulate of continuous variation in nature, Marshall's *natura non facit saltum*. There are degrees of pollution and the relevant decision is rarely either-

M. Mason Gaffney, *professor of economics at the University of Wisconsin— Milwaukee, has a long-standing interest in problems of the environment and contributed a chapter to the recent report of the Air Conservation Commission of the American Association for the Advancement of Science, of which he was a member. He has taught also at the universities of Missouri and Oregon and at North Carolina State College and is the author of numerous monographs and articles for journals and general magazines. Mr. Gaffney was born in 1923 at White Plains, New York. He received his B.A. from Reed College and his Ph.D. from the University of California (Berkeley).*

or, but how much. He points out that the economists' criterion of how much—that is, the optimal balance point where marginal costs equal marginal benefits—applies to pollution control as much as it does to producing apples and oranges.

In benefits and costs he explicitly includes direct effects on human beings, and rejects a narrow concept of economics which would limit its scope to benefits and costs which are detectable through property. He also moves beyond what might be called myopic marginal analysis, with its danger of suboptimization—that is, the danger of moving to the top of a molehill in preference to the shoulder of a mountain—and declares that sometimes we should pass over small-scale measures in favor of large ones like aeration of entire rivers.

A corollary of marginal analysis is that land rents, and land values capitalized therefrom, are useful measurements of the net social benefits of pollution control outlays which are confined within a defined area. One important branch of the Hamlet School of Indecision is the Omelet School of those who tell us one cannot unscramble production and impute specific credits to specific outlays. Mr. Kneese answers the Omelet School argument effectively by pointing out that increments to land rent represent and measure the benefits of pollution control in an area net of the associated costs of taking advantage of them.

Another implication of marginal analysis which Mr. Kneese carries through is that price, in the form of an effluent charge, may serve to constrain pollution, and the constraints have properties in many ways superior to direct controls. Price lets us impose an incremental control, a penalty which is graduated to the severity of the offense and which compensates society for damage to the extent that damage is done.

Along with this missionary work, Mr. Kneese manifests an admirable comprehensiveness and balance in his approach to control measures. One benefit of the effluent charge approach to pollution control is that it leaves the choice of control technique to the individual, thus allowing him a wide range of means to achieve the desired end. Mr. Kneese sees that, in a larger view, the effluent charge approach itself is one of several social techniques to achieve the basic end of pollution control, and he is entirely willing to select the best of the group of control techniques.

He points out that control at the point of effluent discharge may be more costly than control before or after. Another option which he suggests we consider is stream specialization in sewage disposal; that is, letting one stream carry all the sewage of a region so that many streams may be pure. I surmise that he would also approve of neighborhood specialization in noisy and smoky industries and perhaps of regional specialization in crops requiring large use of pesticides, and so on. It would have been useful for him to specify circumstances and offer examples wherein specialization would be desirable.

I further applaud Mr. Kneese's consistent admixture of fact with theory. He does not impose on our time solving imaginary problems for the delectation of those to whom solving problems has become an end in itself. His factually grounded approach draws us to where the productivity of economists' efforts can be at a maximum. He appeals to us, therefore, as concerned citizens with a heavier load of problems to solve than we have the capacity to handle, and who appreciate some help in giving priority to the more consequential problems.

The data which he gives us on pesticides, while fragmentary, shed more light and hope on this gloomy problem than is to be detected in all the jeremiads or the stuffy defensive replies which they have inspired. In the midst of the controversy Mr. Kneese appears *ex machina* with the good old principle of diminishing returns. We don't have to stop using pesticides; we only need to use less. We don't have to let the bugs win; we can use alternative controls instead of so much poison.

His data on the cost of treating municipal drinking water again strike a note of realism in a field often marked by panic and irrationality. San Francisco years ago insisted on importing water over 178 miles from the Sierras in preference to the lower Sacramento, allegedly because of quality preference. Yet that same city not long ago had to be warned by the U.S. Public Health Service that its municipal water was contaminated by leaks in the local distribution system. Millions to grab remote waters, but little concern over quality maintenance at home: can it be that municipal complaints about polluted waters are often a subterfuge for hydro-imperialism?

I applaud Mr. Kneese's emphasis on measurement. It shows that he means business. Abstract theorists who feel they might prejudice their scientific purity by stepping out into the brawl forget, I think, the old aphorism that "science is measurement." Economic measurements are made out in the brawl—they are part of the brawl. But Gentleman Jim Corbett made a science of brawling, after all; economists must do no less.

Mr. Kneese in the space at his disposal could not point to all the gaps that research needs to fill, and I should like to suggest some others.

External Pecuniary Economies. In 1950 the question of secondary benefits, or external pecuniary economies, was regarded as the least well developed question in benefit-cost analysis. It remains so today. The American mind is an engineering mind and easily grasps the reality of technological spillovers like air and water pollution. It requires some conceptualization to see the reality of pecuniary spillovers, and to the concrete mind what is merely abstract is only imaginary.

Yet if Boeing wins a contract from Lockheed all kinds of secondary benefits move to Seattle along with it. Nothing imaginary about that! Many communities have gotten the point. Many of them welcome even polluting industries to secure the associated payroll and tax base.

Not all communities do. Much depends on their finances. Quality of air and water are what economists call "superior goods," that is, goods which command a higher percentage of higher incomes. "Cleanliness is next to affluence," in Thor Hultgren's words. Wealthy suburbs zone out industry, even while blue-collar suburbs and remote towns vie with each other to capture some. But the latter consciously sacrifice environmental quality for money, by choice.

The choice is not always well informed. We should be able to work out more intelligently discriminating ways to compensate industries that generate secondary benefits. Perhaps we could be less avaricious in our eagerness to get net fiscal benefits from them, and in return require greater cleanliness. In any case, we need to put a value on secondary benefits in order to frame any such policies intelligently.

Taxation and the Price System. More analysis of how tax policy affects the price system is needed if we are to use the price system to control pollution, or anything else. If effluent charges are imposed to constrain pollution emissions these would surely be deductible from taxable incomes. The force of the constraint would then vary with the income tax position of each company and individual.

Again, if equipment to control pollution is deductible for federal income tax and if it adds nothing to taxable income then it is already being subsidized, the subsidy again varying with the tax position of the firm or the individual.

The implication of these two points is that to the extent we have already distorted the price system as an index of alternatives we are forced to look to direct controls in preference to price-like controls in order to achieve optimal results. I should prefer to see the price system perfected as a true index of alternatives, but it will be worth using only if it is restored to good working order.

When we use land-value increments and decrements as measures of environmental enhancement or worsening, we are measuring only part, usually less than half, of the value of the environmental change. This is because real estate is subject to taxation, and what we call land value is capitalized from that portion of income which is privately collected and does not reflect the present value of the portion which is publicly collected. In an urban renewal project, for instance, we find the city is more concerned with selling to someone who will pay heavy taxes in the future than it is in selling to someone who will bid the most for the title to the land: the present value of future taxes is greater than the present value of future net ground rent as measured by land value. So if we let land-value increments be the measure of the benefits of pollution control, we understate the pecuniary benefits by a wide margin. On the other hand, we also sneak in a questionable and really quite violent assumption that benefits realized by a minority—the landowners—are a "social" benefit at all. Unearned increments to a few tend to divide society into haves and have-nots and so may do more over-all harm than good. This last question, too, deserves more attention than it has received in many years. That brings us to the matter which classical economists regard as the core of economics, distribution.

Distribution. The question of distributive equity also needs to be an integral part of the economics of pollution abatement. Mr. Kneese's neglect of this question may relate to his underemphasis on institutions. Institutions exist not only to get things done, but to distribute the benefits and levy the costs without which nothing gets done. The following are some of the distributive questions that economists need to answer:

1. Suppose we choose to use large-scale works, like Mr. Kneese's air-injection example, which yield no direct revenue from users. Who then is the beneficiary and who should pay?

2. If we levy an effluent charge, and so earn a surplus, how would we distribute it?

3. If we choose the option of stream specialization and let one stream become a sewer so that others may be pristine, how shall we then compensate the sewer riparians and other beneficiaries? That problem society has hardly ever solved. That is one reason why we make so little use of the principle of stream and area specialization, and instead impose a great gray homogenized mediocrity on all streams.

4. Distributive equity also relates to efficiency. We can hardly achieve efficient resource use without some care in distribution of the income from use. Some economists, from John Stuart Mill to the present, have sought to separate distribution from production and allocation economics. But the market mechanism requires a close correspondence between giving and getting. Income is the motive to produce. If favored landowners get something for nothing, others are probably getting nothing for something, an arrangement that demotivates both. The successful operation of the price system presupposes that it key income to output. Economists need to work on problems of income distribution in order to enhance the efficiency with which the market allocates resources.

Beyond that, many of us question counting the income and unearned increments of a few landowners as part of a social welfare measurement. I have already mentioned their divisiveness. And it is a sterile materialism that asks only what we get and disregards how we get it—why else is larceny unacceptable, the dole demoralizing, and aid without trade self-defeating? Probably the answer lies in having government recover in taxes a larger share of its spending, which raises rents and land values. Then the increase of land rent—publicly collected—could indeed be regarded as a "social" benefit.

5. The distribution of benefits of pollution control also affects the political and ethical rationale for control. Water pollution control, for example, benefits downstream riparian landowners primarily. The ownership of downstream riparian lands is often, even usually, concentrated in a few strong hands. In this circumstance, effluent control may benefit the affluent at the expense of the more politically influential majority. That is politically unattractive and helps account for the unchecked advance of pollution on many waters.

Similarly, on many lakes a few hold the shoreline closely. The public has access from one or two points to the water surface, so most water users have no *pied-à-terre*. This inhibits the development of responsibility among water users, who remain strangers and sojourners in an alien place. If we look forward to a future in which private feelings of common responsibility will take care of most policing problems, we need wide distribution of property.

Concentration of ownership not only means that the distribution of benefits is narrow, but it may often lessen the aggregate value. For example, that would be the case if concentration of riparian land were due to large-tract zoning or to other legal barriers which frustrated the market's demand for subdivision. Concentration of riparian lands may also be traced to tax-motivated preference for capital gains that accrues over ordinary income, which tends to keep land from one who otherwise would be the highest bidder. An equally or more potent "locked-in effect" is created by the provision that exempts entirely from income tax capital gain occurring before the death of an owner who leaves land to heirs without selling it. Sometimes inadequate subdivision of riparian lands is due to imperfections in the credit market which prevent the highest and best users from bidding high enough to get land from an ancient possessor with a low internal rate of time-preference. In these cases the benefits of pollution control are a good deal less than they might be if the land were more widely and economically distributed.

6. Finally, there is a distributive question which we may call the Coase Problem in recognition of Professor R. Coase, who has given it

his attention. Should we regard polluters always as the guilty parties and receptors as injured? Or would it be equally just to say, in the event that pollution is not allowed, that those who enjoy clean air and water are imposing on those who would like to use air and water for waste disposal? If so, what is the *status quo* from which we start? Who should pay whom for doing or not doing what?

If this problem is not solved rationally I believe I can predict what will happen. We will settle on the least justifiable solution of all, that is, priority of occupation. We will say that if the polluters were there first, then pollution is ancient and honorable and no later intruder can complain about it even though the area's best use would be for a TB sanatorium; and contrariwise if a residential use is once established in an area ideally suited by nature as the community's garbage dump, then the community will have to dump its garbage elsewhere at whatever cost to all concerned. To avoid such monstrous results we need some scale of priority other than seniority.

Economics of Space. We should not dissipate our resources in trying to enhance environmental quality equally over all the earth. We need to concentrate our efforts where they will do the most good to people. One important option in pollution control is, for example, not to process wastes as they are removed from centers of population.

Again, how should effluent charges vary with location of the outfall? Presumably upstream polluters should pay more than downstream polluters since their wastes degrade a longer reach of the stream. We need to work out formulas for the variation of effluent charges with location.

A more general question has to do with sewer charges levied on users of a common system. Collecting sewage for treatment is on the whole costlier than treating it. The user at the end of the line imposes much higher costs on the collection system than the user next to the treatment plant. A graduated system of rates needs to be applied, not in a punitive spirit, but with the constructive aim of encouraging a closer congregation of economic activity inside a sewer system in order to minimize collection costs. More positively, that means to maximize the number of dischargers who can be located within a system at reasonable cost.

One of the primary reasons why pollution is getting so far out of hand is urban sprawl, which locates more and more residents or plants outside the reach of existing sewers, and at densities too low to permit of new systems. To the extent that existing systems do reach the new settlement it is by bleeding and neglecting their own centers. They spend their limited money extending lines to reach as many new settlements as possible, deferring needed replacement and enlargement of lines serving older settled areas.

This leads to a more general question of spatial economics, settlement density. In order to achieve scale economies in treating effluents before discharge into a river we need to have all polluters located close together to share the cost of a common facility. Mr. Kneese's discussion of large-scale treatment is limited to the treatment of whole rivers after discharge of pollutants. This is no criticism, he could not discuss everything; but the most relevant economy of scale is the economy of collective sewage treatment, which only becomes possible when large numbers of waste generators can share the cost of a common treatment plant.

Modern Americans thoughtlessly tried to escape from the pollution which we rather vaguely associate with the city by running half-way back to the country. Some call exurbia a happy medium, but in pollution matters it is the worst of both worlds. People can get along at low rural density, where they are far enough apart not to pollute each other's water; and again at high urban density where close enough to use common facilities. But on the sprawling urban fringe we are close enough to get in each other's way and too far apart to do anything about it. The number of contaminated wells found each year is a material and growing percentage of the whole. If we could or would afford to check each small private well regularly, and if public officials dared release the results, we might be shocked at what we have been drinking in this modern sanitary age and we might pinpoint one important cause of impaired human function and health.

Rather than an expansion of exurban living we need a means for quick and complete transition of land from rural to urban density. The dynamics of urban expansion are of the essence. Septic tanks that seem workable when the first few dwellings dot an area begin to overload the underground capacity as the area fills in, and various unpleasantnesses ensue. Large minimum lot size seems to help, but also makes a sewer network prohibitively costly—$1,200 per lot is a recent figure from exurban Milwaukee. The low density for which the community is originally planned proves unworkable; the leap to workable high density is too great for the exurbanite's psychology to face and accept; so exurbia careens from expedient to expedient and what might have been an orderly supersession becomes a nightmare of conflict, tension, and waste.

These remarks barely scratch the surface of a question of infinite fascination and paramount importance. Most questions of environmental quality involve settlement density: the cost of environmental enhancement rises with area, and its value with population. In general, that means the higher the settlement density, the higher quality of physical environment we can afford to maintain.

High density in some areas is also the best guarantee of low density in other areas. If people live here, they needn't live there. We can let some areas specialize in accommodating large numbers of people at a high level of environmental quality, and others in receiving garbage, pollution, and debris, with very few people. That should leave most of the world more or less "natural," which some, less tasty than I to mosquitoes, regard as the highest quality environment of all. But we cannot afford to maintain uniform high standards throughout the whole world, and we need to give high priority to analysis and policy making on the question of when and where not to try.

Unexplored Alternatives. Some alternative means of pollution control worthy of attention are the following:

1. We can export pollution by importing products whose manufacture or mining pollute the environment. Sugar, which Mr. Kneese discusses, is something we should be importing anyway from tropical nations because they produce at lower cost, even if we exclude the external (to the firm) cost of polluting water. Add to that, most tropical nations are more willing to accept pollution because of sparser population and lower per capita wealth. Some people may not care to talk out loud about the last point for fear of igniting flammable tropical inferiority complexes by appearing condescending. Yet if trade is a "voluntary act between consenting adults," where lies the condescension? It is refusing foreign sugar that really provokes resentment, and to do so on the pretext that we are protecting our little brothers from pollution that they might prefer if we allowed them free choice would add condescension and hypocrisy to injury.

The same argument applies to petroleum. Why not let the Sheik of Kuwait suffer the pollution associated with oil wells? He might appreciate the option, and we should be getting our oil from the lowest cost source anyway.

2. The heavy use of pesticides which we now suffer is, as Mr. Kneese points out, in part a substitution of pesticide for land, and might be alleviated by substituting land for pesticide. Since the U.S. Department of Agriculture has 60 million acres or so in programs of the soil bank type, would it not make more sense, if we insist on limiting farm output, to do so instead by cutting back on pesticides? It doesn't make much sense to hold all that land in cold storage anyway.

Along the same line, we could produce our present domestic output of oil with one-half or less the present number of wells if we let the superior wells produce thirty days a month instead of holding them down to seven or eight days a month as we do now and letting only the marginal stripper wells produce constantly. When we see oil rigs disfiguring the landscape, and marginal mines polluting water, let us not blame it on economics, or laissez-faire, or other conventional scapegoats. A large part of the landscape disfigurement which mineral extraction imposes does not result from economic necessity at all, but from sheer boondoggling inherent in the prorate or allowable system. The economist who would like to rationalize the oil industry needs to join forces with the environmentalist who would like to preserve the landscape. They have a common interest in substituting a few superior wells and mines for many marginal ones.

3. It would be useful to modify our property tax and income tax policies so as to accelerate the replacement of obsolete equipment. Much air and water pollution comes from ancient ineffective plants which enjoy grandfather-clause protection in their polluting activities. Tax policies to accelerate replacement of such antiquities would be desirable on other grounds. When we add the feature of environmental quality the case here should be irresistible except to those who regard antiquity itself as the highest feature of environmental quality.

Market Structure. We need to study the effectiveness of effluent charges under conditions of imperfect competition. The rationale as developed so far presupposes competitive markets, and to the extent that that is not true the results might fall short of perfection. An effluent charge paid by a monopolist might have less effect than the same charge levied on a competitive firm.

Institutional Economics. Environmental quality demands more economic research on social institutions. Mr. Kneese has emphasized that economists need to bend their analyses to engineering constraints. But institutional constraints can be equally compelling. The cost of amending the United States Constitution or a state constitution, of reversing a common-law rule or a precedent *stare decisis,* or altering established *mores,* may be high enough to prohibit all manner of otherwise useful ideas. The social institutions hammered out through centuries of human trial and error are real facts of the world, every bit as controlling as physical facts.

There is a danger of forgetting that institutions are means rather than ends. Institutional economics does not imply institutional idolatry, either open or in its thin disguise of taxonomy. Let economists continue to criticize obsolete and ill-conceived institutions which block economic adjustments. But let them do more than remove blockades; they must build channels for positive social action. The development of effective, workable social institutions like California's Irrigation Districts was, as

Albert Henley put it, ". . . of infinitely more value to California than the discovery of gold a generation earlier."

It is a truism that institutional evolution is far behind science and engineering. It seems to follow that the marginal productivity of economists' time would be highest if directed to designing institutions.

That certainly was my experience working with water law and economics in California. Why should economists elaborate models of optimal allocation and programming of water, fuss over finer points of theory, when water law may not let one move water across the street from a swamp to a desert? As Professor Boulding has observed, an engineer then becomes someone who figures the very best way to do something that shouldn't be done at all.

On the positive side, California is rich in constructive enabling legislation. California law authorizes local citizens to set up special districts that can do everything but stand on their heads. California and other states have districts for drainage, flood control, air pollution control, mosquito abatement, sanitation, water conservation, weed control, etc., *ad infinitum*. These adjudicated precedents bear close study by American economists—more, probably, than German precedents—for they are the institutional mechanism most readily available for environmental control without performing major surgery on federal and state constitutions, and without waiting through years or decades of jeopardy of judicial review.

Medical Research. We do not know the marginal contribution of pollution to death and disease. That is one of the most important things we need to learn. Mr. Kneese gently intimates that M.D.'s could contribute more to guiding public policy on these matters if they would use some of the economists' marginal concepts in framing their research. I would like to shout, where he has whispered, that much medical research and thinking are monumentally irrelevant to public policy decisions because of the profession's inability to submit its findings to the common discipline and comparison implicit in marginal analysis. Yet if it did mount a greater effort to communicate in a common tongue it might very well be, as Mr. Kneese suggests, that the relative importance of medical discipline would be enhanced.

There is little in Mr. Kneese's paper with which to take direct issue. That, indeed, is my first criticism—the language is often guarded, the meaning open to inference.

Second, I would object to the overuse of the first person plural. The antecedents of Mr. Kneese's "we" evolve in a somewhat misleading way

He confesses early that his survey of research is partly autobiographical but the emphasis soon evolves from self to Resources for the Future, and as he warms to the topic he increasingly gives the impression that "we" comprises most people who matter.

I would not quibble over the stylistic point, but it reflects a state of mind that may mislead one. For example, Mr. Kneese says that the benefit-cost analysis used in water policy is "the most advanced field of applied welfare economics." I think what he means by that is that a few economists have written good books on the subject; but I see little evidence that those books have stopped the Arkansas or the Feather River projects. On the contrary, these boondoggles are now dwarfed by the incredible nonsense of a proposal, seriously advanced, to carry water from Alaska to California. "We" may know better, but another "we" flow on to decision unvexed by "our" wisdom.

Again, the idea that the benefits of environmental enhancement show up in increased land values may be news to "us" economists, but it has been preached vigorously from every real estate sales office in the Western world from at least the days of the South Sea Bubble, and has long been the effective criterion used by many local governments to decide on outlays for school, fire, police, street lights, utility extensions, etc.

Yet again, I think Mr. Kneese overstates the novelty of studies of damage to downstream users of degraded water. The California Department of Water Resources and related agencies have monitored water quality for years. Downstream irrigators have had upstream users in court for generations and the constant fussing has generated volumes of information. All of that is known to some people, even if it is not part of that restricted literature which we sometimes refer to as the main body of economic knowledge.

A third criticism is that Mr. Kneese overdifferentiates his subject. Most government services are designed to improve the quality of the environment in one way or another. Economic techniques designed to evaluate the benefits of fire protection, garbage collection, pest and contagion control, street lighting, drainage, and even police work are transferable and partially applicable to evaluate pollution control measures. Thus Mr. Kneese overstates our profession's neglect of environmental quality studies. It is the more specific application to pollution control that has languished.

True, economists have far to go in evaluating the benefits of public goods. But Mr. Kneese might have cited a great deal of work in marginal cost pricing, on layout of distribution, and collection grids (like sewers), on vertical summation of demand curves for public goods, on pay T.V., on the value of weather information, etc.[1] Still there remains a bite in Mr. Kneese's implied criticism. Economists for the most part have simply been talking to each other on these matters. We deserve to be faulted for too little effort to reach a consensus and then to shout it from the housetops. Mr. Kneese deserves high praise for his success in wider communication.

Fourth, I detect hints that Mr. Kneese is too easy on polluters. Concerning pesticides, there is "no evidence of any effect." That phrase implies to me he puts the burden of proof on the damaged person. I suggest it belongs on the polluter. The Food and Drug Administration requires the seller to prove safeness before distributing a new drug. In the case of polluters the case is even stronger because their neighbors' exposure is involuntary.

Where measurement and proof are tenuous, as with many pollutants, placing the burden of proof may be a paramount issue. I would not want 100 per cent of the burden on the polluters. Some rule of reason needs to apply—another institutional problem. Making change too burdensome is a tool of blind conservatism. But I do think Mr. Kneese's statement suggests a greater tolerance of those who would use the rest of us as guinea pigs than I find acceptable.

Again, he suggests that imperfect knowledge may inhibit us from controlling pollution. But put the burden of proof on polluters, and

---

[1] A partial list of relevant literature follows: Burton A. Weisbrod, "Collective Consumption Services of Individual Consumption Goods," *Quarterly Journal of Economics,* August 1964, pp. 471–77. Julius Margolis, "Metropolitan Finance Problems: Territories, Functions, and Growth," *Public Finances: Needs, Sources, and Utilization,* National Bureau of Economic Research (Princeton: Princeton University Press, 1961), pp. 229–70. Carl S. Shoup, "Standards for Distributing a Free Governmental Service: Crime Prevention," *Public Finances/Finances Publiques,* XIX (4), 1964, pp. 383–92. A. G. Holtman, "Estimating the Demand for Public Health Services: The Alcoholism Case," *Public Finances/Finances Publiques,* XIX (4), 1964, pp. 351–58. Werner Z. Hirsch, "Cost Functions of an Urban Government Service: Refuse Collection," *Review of Economics and Statistics,* February 1965, pp. 87–92. Charles M. Tiebout, "A Pure Theory of Local Expenditures," *Journal of Political Economy,* October 1956, pp. 416–24; "An Economic Theory of Fiscal Decentralization," *Public Finances: Needs, Sources, and Utilization,* National Bureau of Economic Research (Princeton: Princeton University Press, 1961), pp. 76–96. James M. Buchanan, "Private Ownership and Common Usage: The Road Case Reexamined," *Southern Economic Journal,* January 1956, pp. 305–16. J. Tinbergen, "The Appraisal of Road Construction: Two Calculated Schemes," *Review of Economics and Statistics,* August 1957, pp. 241–49. Lester B. Lave, "The Value of Better Weather Information for the Raisin Industry," *Econometrica,* January-April 1963, pp. 151–64. Jora Minasian, "Television Pricing and the Theory of Public Goods," *Journal of Law and Economics,* October 1964. R. Dorfman (ed.), *Measuring Benefits of Government Investments* (Washington: The Brookings Institution, 1965).

imperfect knowledge would prevent our permitting any pollution! In fact, no legislature has ever possessed perfect knowledge. Society must always contrive to act on the basis of what is known. Where reasonable doubt remains about the safety of new pollutants, I would be inclined to check their use tightly until those who profit from their sale and use have managed to demonstrate safety.

Finally, the phrase "environmental quality" is too comprehensive really to describe the specific concerns covered in Mr. Kneese's paper. The environment of slum dwellers consists largely of houses and streets, joints and cheap stores, playgrounds and schools, garbage cans and vibrations from neighborhood drop-forges. Perhaps it would be well to attend more to such more intimate urban environmental matters. Ameliorating them can improve the lot of man by a larger factor than cleaning up lakes used by summer sportsmen of the wealthier classes or improving the scenery on which they occasionally gaze with cultivated eyes. Meantime, the present subject is better called "pollution control and aesthetic uplift from the viewpoint of the upper-middle classes."

On balance, these criticisms are minor and I strongly applaud Mr. Kneese's paper. He applies economic theory to practical problems, and does it very well, contrary to the all-too-common habit among scholars of segregating theory and practice. The universities turn out our idealists and theoreticians, and then our nuts-and-bolts practitioners, and never the twain shall meet. By blending theory and practice so well, Mr. Kneese enhances not just the physical but the intellectual environmental quality of his times.

The intellectual environment in turn affects the social and psychological environments, which touch us as deeply as the physical. Improving the physical world improves the improver; reaching harmony of man and nature finds harmony of man and man. Here the means may indeed be the end!

Chapter Five

{ PUBLIC ATTITUDES ON }
{ ENVIRONMENTAL QUALITY }

Gilbert F. White

FORMATION AND ROLE OF PUBLIC ATTITUDES

At the heart of managing a natural resource is the manager's perception of the resource and of the choices open to him in dealing with it. At the heart of decisions on environmental quality are a manager's views of what he and others value in the environment and can preserve or cultivate. This is not a conclusion. It is a definition: natural resources are taken to be culturally defined, decisions are regarded as choices among perceived alternatives for bringing about change, and any choice presumes a view of the resource together with preferences in outcome and methods.

Little can be said by way of conclusion as to how the public's evaluation of environment and methods does in fact affect the decisions which are reached in polluting air and water, or defacing the terrain, or destroying habitat or in efforts to prevent or repair such damage. The terms themselves are slithery. Pollution or defacement of a physical landscape can only be measured against a human preference. Human perception

Gilbert F. White *has been professor of geography at the University of Chicago since 1956. For the ten years before that he was president of Haverford College. Previously he had been on the staffs of the Mississippi Valley Committee, the National Resources Committee and the National Resources Planning Board. He was a member of the Hoover Commission task force on natural resources in 1948, vice chairman of the President's Water Resources Policy Commission in 1950, and chairman of the United Nations Panel on Integrated River Development in 1957–58. Since 1964 he has been chairman of the National Academy of Sciences Committee on Water. He is the author of* Human Adjustment to Floods *and* Science and the Future of Arid Lands *and of numerous monographs and papers. Mr. White was born in Chicago in 1911 and received his S.B. and Ph.D. degrees from the University of Chicago.*

The author is grateful to Wesley C. Calef, Robert W. Kates, W. R. Derrick Sewell, Fred L. Strodtbeck, and Meda M. White for critical comments on an earlier draft of this paper.

and preference are related to environment and personality in ways which are not well explored. Much of the public discussion is masked by a rough plaster of horseback judgments that hide the structure of action and opinion formation. The difficulties, pitfalls, and opportunities are illustrated in a recent decision by a community of 50,000 people.

The voters of Boulder, Colorado, went to the polls in July 1965, to cast their ballots for or against two proposals certain to alter the environment which they will occupy in the years ahead. One was authorization for a bond issue to pay for construction of an additional sewage disposal plant to reduce the waste that the rapidly growing city pours into Boulder Creek below its municipal limits. The second was to approve an agreement under which city water would be delivered to a mesa south of the city, and thus permit residential invasion of a high, scenic sector of the piedmont adjoining the Rocky Mountain front. Voting was desultory, the totals were close, but the practical outcome was plain. The treatment plant gained approval, the water extension met defeat.

To understand how these decisions were reached and how public attitudes influenced them would require answers to a series of questions beyond the voting returns. The answers needed for Boulder exemplify those needed wherever public agencies alter environment. What is the decision-making network in Boulder, not only as it shows in the electoral decision but in the public and citizen agencies that framed the issues and sought to influence public action? What attitudes toward water quality and landscape enjoyment were held by those who took any part in the decision? How did their attitudes shape the public choice? What factors affect these attitudes? To what extent and in what circumstances are the attitudes subject to change? These questions will be reviewed in a broader context at the close of this paper.

The Boulder decisions were relatively simple in the concreteness of the issues, the number of people taking part, and the narrow area affected.

Consider the difficulty of trying to understand the genesis and implications of a declaration from the Department of the Interior[1] that:

Slowly, there is dawning in man an understanding of the intertwined cause and effect pattern which makes him subject, in some small way, to every slightest tampering with his total environment. If he is to enjoy the fruits of a truly Great Society, he must be willing to work for quality everywhere, not just in his own back yard; he must consider not just the fumes from his own car, but the total exhaust cloud from the Nation's vehicles;

[1] *Quest for Quality*: U.S. Department of the Interior Conservation Yearbook (Washington: U.S. Government Printing Office, 1965), p. 13.

he must wonder not just where the next drink of water is coming from, but what is being done to keep the world's taps from going dry.

How is it known what is dawning on man, and what is the quality he enjoys? Some observers argue that a consensus is emerging as to what is good quality in the environment. Looking to problems of policy formation, Caldwell argues:

> The need for a generalizing concept of environmental development that will provide a common denominator among differing values and interests is becoming clearer. And the concept of "good" environment, however one defines it, is certainly no less concrete, tangible, and specific than the concepts of freedom, prosperity, security, and welfare that have on various occasions served to focus public policy.[2]

How can these felt needs be recognized and weighed? How do they or should they affect public decision? In what ways may they be expected to change?

The number of people and organized groups directly involved in decisions that affect the quality of environment can be stated with some accuracy for any area. Water management to alter the water cycle in the United States provides one example. It is known that approximately 306,000 farmers irrigate land independently or through 8,750 districts, that farmers organized in 8,460 districts drain off excess water from the land, that 18,150 incorporated urban governments provide water and dispose of it for their residents, that each of 7,720 manufacturing plants withdraw on the average more than 20 millions of gallons of water daily for industrial purposes, that agencies and organizations generate hydroelectric power at 1,600 plants, that at least 3,700,000 rural homeowners provide their own water and waste disposal facilities, that every one of the farmers affects the movement of water on and in the soil, and that numerous state and federal agencies exercise some kind of influence over these choices.

For each of the direct decisions to make or not make one of these alterations in hydrologic systems there may be presumed to be a network of relationships. Where one manager is directly involved, as with a farmer who decides to install his own septic tank, his choice may be influenced only by a county sanitary requirement, by technical information supplied by state agencies and local merchants, and by the expressed preferences of his neighbors. Where an organization is involved, the whole process is complicated by the character of internal choice and by

---

[2] Lynton K. Caldwell, "Environment: A New Focus for Public Policy?", *Public Administration Review* (1965), p. 138.

the number of exterior conditions that influence the process. Networks for decisions to modify air, vegetation, and urban landscape are even more complex.

Adequate models are lacking to describe the intricacies of decision making and, thereby, to indicate critical points in the process. There seems no doubt that an individual manager of a sector of the environment takes into account in some fashion the range of possible uses, the character of the environment itself, the technology available to him for using the environment, and the expected gains and losses to himself and others from the possible action. His perception and judgment at each point is bound to occur in a framework of habitual behavior and of social guidance exercised through constraints or incentives. When the decision is lodged in an organization there is added the strong motivation of its members to seek equilibrium and to preserve the organization while accommodating its structure to changes required by shifts in preferences, environment, or personnel.[3]

Just how much of a role attitudes play in the final outcome is a matter for speculation at present. Little evidence is in hand. A few case studies of decision making suggest points at which they might be expected to be especially significant. Thus, Gore's examination of selected government operations suggests that "formal organization accounts for only a part of surface behavior," and that informal organization, with its sensitivity to motivation, communication, sanction, habituated behavior, and threat symbol, help explain the remainder.[4] Certainly, individual goals and beliefs figure importantly in the organizational behavior.

Less systematic observations of the course of environmental management show a few obviously critical situations. Early efforts to develop public water supplies in the United States encountered serious inertia because many people did not believe in the germ theory of disease: until attitudes toward disease were altered proponents of the new, more sanitary supplies had hard sledding. A large city electric utility corporation recently installed precipitators in the stacks of a thermal fuel plant because it thought conspicuous smoke plumes would impair its relations with its customers. The classic case in the water field is the decision of the Board of Water Supply of New York City in the 1950's to pass over further study of the Hudson River as a water source because of its belief that the water-users would object to anything other than pure, upland sources.

Attitudes enter into decisions in three ways. First, there are personal

[3] Herbert Simon and J. March, *Organizations* (New York: John Wiley and Sons, 1958).

[4] William J. Gore, *Administrative Decision-Making: A Heuristic Model* (New York: John Wiley and Sons, 1964).

attitudes of the people sharing in the decision. Second, are their opinions as to what others prefer. Third, are their opinions as to what others should prefer. The three need not, and rarely do coincide, although there probably is a tendency for personal and normative attitudes to merge. In Boulder, an influential citizen favored a clean stream, thought that most of his fellows did not, and urged them to adopt waste treatment. Another Boulderite regarded the mesa subdivision as an abomination, thought his fellows did not, and supported a negative vote against it. In a national park not far away, a government official who would prefer to walk and camp in a sector where no roads are present or may be seen, ignored his own preferences in advocating a new highway which would gash the mountain slopes in making the landscape accessible to tourists who, he believed, like it that way. The Outdoor Recreation Resources Review Commission was the first public agency to attempt an orderly canvass of consumer demand for qualitative use of environment, and it was careful in reporting the findings as to trends in outdoor recreation to note "A projection of these trends cannot foretell the future, but there are important clues here indicating the new order of needs."[5]

The literature of resources management and conservation is rife with assertions of what the people want. These range from sweeping declarations that "So far, our history has recorded two great threats, or attitudes, with relation to our natural resources, and now we are beginning a third,"[6] to closely-reasoned arguments that the government actions in a democratic society reflect the ultimate resolution of conflicting preferences.

Far more influential in the daily course of environmental modification is the assessment of public attitudes that goes unsung and largely unrecorded. This is the assessment that is lodged deep in the engineering design of a new Potomac River dam or in the administrative decision to specify standards for land use in a Cascades wilderness. An engineer judges that people will be satisfied with a given taste of water or with a certain monotony of wayside design or with a stream bank that is deprived of algae growth. Once plowed into a design or office memorandum, the assumption may never reappear in its original seminal form, but it may bear profuse fruit in the character of daily action.

Strictly speaking, there is no single expert opinion about attitudes toward quality of environment; there are the opinions each person holds, the opinions he thinks others hold, and the opinions he thinks they should hold. Many public administrators get mixed up about this. Perhaps the greatest confusion arises from their not knowing what others

[5] *Outdoor Recreation for America,* U.S. Outdoor Recreation Resources Review Commission (Washington: U.S. Government Printing Office, 1962), p. 27.
[6] *Quest for Quality, op. cit.,* p. 6.

do believe and from lacking means of finding out. What follows is a preliminary attempt to outline what is known and not known about attitudes toward quality of environment and the ways in which they vary from person to person, place to place, and time to time.

Before touching on some of what is known and not known about attitudes affecting environmental decisions, caution should be offered at four points. The first and basic reservation is that the analysis is made by a geographer who, while seeking help from social psychologist colleagues, has not absorbed their scientific lore, and who reports the use of their conclusions but may not fully comprehend the grounds for them. During the past year a few social psychologists and geographers at the University of Chicago have joined under an RFF grant in an exploration of attitudes towards water.[7] Much of what follows stems from that investigation, especially the remaining cautions.

The term "attitude" is used interchangeably with "belief" or "opinion" to describe a preference held by a person with respect to an object or concept. It does not in itself constitute a value or mark of value; it is the result of a valuation process of some kind, and always involves a preference. Insofar as it applies to an aspect of the environment it requires perception of that environment. By perception is meant the individual organization of sensory stimulation.[8] Apparently, there is no perception which is not organized on the basis of social experience. All of the evidence indicates that the same mountain landscape may be perceived quite differently by two people, to one as lowering and ominous, to another as refreshing and uplifting; that one man honestly terms clean a stream which another labels dirty; and that the same size coin looks larger to one boy than to another.[9] A common feature of perception is distortion of unfamiliar phenomena to adjust to familiar orientation, as when a geometrically minded American sees a skewed window frame in a different perspective in order to make it appear rectilinear. Or it may obscure painful reactions, as when a loving father does not observe a marring twist in a daughter's face. The term cognitive dissonance, as

[7] The report currently is in preparation under the title of *Attitudes Toward Water: An Interdisciplinary Exploration*. Principal participants have been Fred L. Strodtbeck, Meda White, William Bezdek, and Don Goldhammer from the Laboratory of Social Psychology, and W. R. Derrick Sewell, David Czamanske and Richard Schmoyer, from the Department of Geography. Several of the cautions as to definition were suggested by Fred Strodtbeck.

[8] David Lowenthal, "Geography, Experience, and Imagination: Towards a Geographical Epistemology," *Annals of the Association of American Geographers*, 51 (1961), pp. 241–60.

[9] Jerome S. Bruner and Cecile C. Goodman, "Value and Need as Organizing Factors in Perception," *Journal of Abnormal and Social Psychology*, Vol. 42 (1947), pp. 33–44.

used by Festinger, describes the transformation.[10] There can be no thoroughly objective perception of the environment, only degrees of distortion which are minimized in rigorous scientific description. If this is true, then there can be no absolute standards of aesthetic experience, only standards which vary with experience and personality. What is perceived as reality may differ from person to person, and it seems likely that in such elementary ways as viewing abstract designs people vary in their spatial styles, in their preference, for example, of vertical as against horizontal lines.[11]

The next caution is against equating quality of environment with quality of life. When people speak of a high quality of an environmental vista, they often mean that the stimulus which it offers has led to a perception and accompanying response by the viewer which they regard as good for the viewer. The proper test is not the landscape itself but the response of whoever is stimulated by it. The response of an ardent ecologist who is inspired by exposure to an almost wholly undisturbed ecosystem may be like that of a mathematician in reverence before a perfect proof: the object inspires joy in the recognition of something which satisfies a particular human yearning for perfection. If this is true, then it is misleading rather than helpful to distinguish between quality of natural environment and quality of social environment. Quite aside from the fact that virtually no bit of the earth's surface is wholly undisturbed by man, it is important to remember that what commonly is called natural environment has meaning solely in a social setting in which the preferences are those of man interacting with man and nature.

The suggestion that the natural-social distinction be dropped may offend a few environmental engineers, but there is not likely to be solid objection from engineers or architects who attempt to design new buildings and communities. They subscribe in principle to the idea that they are shaping the total environment. The chief difficulty arises in trying to carry out the theory. Thus far, there are no instances where this has been done through rigorous application of what is known about human environmental stimuli.

A final caution has to do with the tendency to explain part of man's use of environment as rational and part as irrational. This is an attractive and convenient dichotomy, particularly when attention is directed toward economic optimization. It is said, for example, that if farmers were rational they would adjust their operations, within whatever constraints

---

[10] Leon Festinger, *A Theory of Cognitive Dissonance* (New York: Harper and Row, 1957).

[11] Robert Beck, "Spatial Meaning, and the Properties of the Environment," in *Environmental Perception and Behavior,* edited by David Lowenthal (Chicago: University of Chicago Geography Research Papers, in press).

are set by social institutions, so as to maximize their net returns. Quite aside from the baffling task of recognizing social incentives and constraints, there are two difficulties in trying to pursue the distinction of rationality. One is that human goals rarely if ever are clearly defined; generally they are ambiguous. There is not a single program or single policy in recent United States resource management that displays a unitary, unambiguous aim. Several aims are fused, and the most ardent administrators revel in the flexibility afforded by the resulting ambiguity: flood control is to save lives and protect economically efficient development; highway beautification is to enhance the landscape and make it more accessible by concrete expressways; waste treatment is to reduce health hazards and to render streams more useful for a variety of purposes. As it is with organizations, so it is with individuals. It is sanguine to expect neat, unambiguous aims and decision criteria.

A second difficulty is that the factors of personality and environment are so complex that to speak of a rational process is to ascribe a clarity of action and observation that rarely is attained. It is enough to struggle for rational, accurate description without seeking or claiming to find rationality in the action itself.

To sum up the cautions: Do not regard this as comprehensive from the standpoint of the social sciences. Remember that every attitude toward environment involves perception that is organized by individuals. Avoid equating quality of life with quality of environment, for the latter is judged only by the former. Abandon any early claims for rationality, and look at the way in which living people behave.

Five different avenues are followed by those who would discover attitudes. They twist and sometimes cross, but rarely merge.

The first and more traditional method is to analyze the interpretations which articulate man has made of his environment. The central route here is scholarly, sensitive appraisal of what man has felt about nature through his writings and his graphic art. Lowenthal gives the most comprehensive introduction to this approach,[12] and Glacken presses it searchingly in his examinations of attitudes toward nature held by scientists and other observers.[13] Tuan has called attention to landscapes

[12] Lowenthal, *op. cit.*
[13] Clarence J. Glacken, "Changing Ideas of the Habitable World," in *Man's Role in Changing the Face of the Earth* (Chicago: University of Chicago Press, 1956), pp. 70–92; and "Man's Attitude Toward Land: Reflections on the Man-Nature Theme as a Subject for Study," in *Future Environments of North America,* the papers of the Conservation Foundation Conference of 1965 (New York: The Natural History Press, 1966). See also Alexander Spoehr, "Cultural Differences in the Interpretation of Natural Resources," in *Man's Role in Changing the Face of the Earth,* pp. 93–102.

which in literature have taken on special symbolic significance.[14] Travel diaries, the notes of explorers, or rock paintings may reveal the terrain as humans observe it.

Content analysis has the same purpose and uses the same material —the written word—but applies a more rigorous method. The Boulder decision can be subjected to analysis by examining the entire printed discussion that preceded the election according to prescribed categories of form, direction, authority, and value.[15] On the water question, the supporters stressed the need for planned development and for improvements which would enhance the city's growth. They argued that the mesa service area would enlarge the tax base, and appealed to the city's reputation and the responsibility of its citizens. Opponents stressed a prospective shortage of water and higher taxes. They argued that the city officials had acted unwisely and that the citizens should concern themselves only with the welfare of the city itself. Generally, the arguments against were not the obverse of those for, and the opposition was oriented around individual cost while support was oriented around community gain. The opposition tended to place more emphasis on effects which could be stated quantitatively than on quality, and to criticize details of design. The printed statements about the sewer issue were similar in character.

An intermediate variant of content analysis is represented by Elson's investigation of more than 1,000 textbooks used in the first eight years of American schooling during the nineteenth century.[16] It leads to the following type of conclusion as to attitudes toward nature:

Thus the nineteenth-century child was taught that nature is animated with man's purposes. God designed nature for man's physical needs and spiritual training. Scientific understanding of nature will reveal the greater glory of God, and the practical application of such knowledge should be encouraged as part of the use God meant man to make of nature. Besides serving the material needs of man, nature is a source of man's health, strength, and virtue. He departs at his peril from a life close to nature. At a time when America was becoming increasingly industrial and urban, agrarian values which had been a natural growth in earlier America became articles of fervent faith in American nationalism. The American character had been formed in virtue because it developed in a rural environment, and it must

[14] Yi-Fu Tuan, "Attitudes Toward Environment: Themes and Approaches," *Environmental Perception and Behavior,* edited by David Lowenthal (Chicago: University of Chicago Geography Research Papers, in Press).

[15] Bernard Berelson, *Content Analysis in Communication Research* (Glencoe: Free Press, 1952). David Czamanske applied this type of analysis to the Boulder data, using material printed in the *Boulder Camera* during one month and compiled by Mary B. White.

[16] Ruth Miller Elson, *Guardians of Tradition: American Textbooks of the Nineteenth Century* (Lincoln: University of Nebraska Press, 1964), pp. 39–40.

remain the same despite vast environmental change. The existence of a bounteous and fruitful frontier in America, with its promise not only of future prosperity but of continued virtue, offers proof that God has singled out the United States above other nations for His fostering care. The superiority of nature to man-made things confers superiority on the American over older civilizations. That Uncle Sam sooner or later will have to become a city dweller is not envisaged by these textbook writers, although their almost fanatical advocacy of rural values would seem to suggest an unconscious fear that this might be so.

All of these appraisals raise the problem of how representative were the artists or pedestrian textbook writers upon whose work they are based. Was Corot's view of the forest in any sense indicative of the attitude of French foresters who managed the state land? Did McGuffey speak for the tillers of soil in Indiana? Were local newspapers which said of the Indiana prairie land in 1830 that the soil was suitable for cultivation a more accurate measure of the contemporary farmer's perception of his environment than the latter day historians who spoke of avoidance of the prairies? McManis shows that they were.[17]

If the artists' interpretation is to be verified, a second course of inquiry is to go directly to the people. Here enters the opinion pollster. An expression of attitude may be solicited by questions, and this may be checked for internal consistency and structure. Beginning with the Department of Agriculture Program Surveys in 1940,[18] the opinion surveys of the National Opinion Research Center[19] and the Center for Survey

---

[17] Douglas R. McManis, *The Initial Valuation and Utilization of the Illinois Prairies, 1815–1840* (Chicago: University of Chicago Geography Research Series, No. 94, 1964), pp. 49–58, 89–95.

[18] The Program Surveys were initiated by farseeing officials and social psychologists who sought to understand more precisely why farmers accepted certain government measures and rejected others, why some were concerned about eroding soil or sustained woodland management and others were not. Political exigencies of the period soon drove the effort into assessment of responses to international policies and wartime controls, and other data collected then has received little notice. It would merit re-examination for its revelations of attitudes prevailing in the 1940's and for its suggestions of factors which then seemed relevant. Comments on the work are to be found in Rensis Likert, "Opinion Studies and Government Policy," *Proceedings of the American Philosophical Society* (1948), pp. 341–50.

[19] Studies published by the National Opinion Research Center involving assessment of environment: Paul N. Borsky, *Community Reactions to Sonic Booms, Oklahoma City Area*, Pt. 1, University of Chicago, National Opinion Research Center, Report No. 101, 1965; Community Conservation Board, City of Chicago, *The Hyde Park–Kenwood Urban Renewal Survey*, University of Chicago, National Opinion Research Center Report No. 58, 1956; and Community Conservation Board, City of Chicago, *The Near West Side Conservation Survey*, University of Chicago, National Opinion Research Center Report No. 63-B, 1957.

Research[20] have canvassed segments of the American population from time to time as to its preferences concerning environment. The most extensive effort, sponsored by the Outdoor Recreational Resources Review Commission, inquired into the current habits of use of outdoor lands, and attempted to forecast the likely shifts in demand which would result from changes in population, income, and transportation.[21] Several recent studies of the survey type dealt with opinions toward air pollution in the Clarkston, Washington,[22] and metropolitan St. Louis areas,[23] and toward aviation noise at an Air Force base.[24] From the array of responses to those surveys it is possible to describe certain articulated attitudes toward environment, ranging from air quality to juvenile delinquency, and to correlate them with social status, location, and views of the community.

Assuming that the samples are representative, complications in the use of results of opinion surveys arise from the degree to which the interview situation reflects conditions which would be at work if the

[20] Studies of the Survey Research Center, Institute for Social Research, University of Michigan, Ann Arbor, published by the Institute unless otherwise noted: Angus Campbell and Charles A. Metzner, *Public Use of the Library and Other Sources of Information,* 1950; Eva L. Mueller and Gerald Gurin, with Margaret Wood, *Participation in Outdoor Recreation: Factors Affecting Demand Among American Adults,* Washington, U.S. Government Printing Office, 1962; Eva L. Mueller, Arnold A. Wilken, and Margaret Wood, *Location Decisions and Industrial Mobility in Michigan, 1961,* 1962; John B. Lansing, Eva L. Mueller, William M. Ladd, and Nancy Barth, *The Geographic Mobility of Labor: A First Report,* 1963; John B. Lansing and Eva L. Mueller, with Nancy (Morse) Samuelson, *Residential Location and Urban Mobility,* 1964; John B. Lansing and Nancy (Morse) Samuelson, *Residential Location and Urban Mobility: A Multivariate Analysis,* 1964; John B. Lansing, Residential Location and Urban Mobility: The Second Wave of Interviews, 1966.

[21] *The Future of Outdoor Recreation in Metropolitan Regions of the United States,* Vol. I, The National View—Present Conditions and Future Prospects of Outdoor Recreation for Residents of the Metropolitan Centers of Atlanta, St. Louis, and Chicago, A Report to the Outdoor Recreation Resources Review Commission, Study Report 21 (Washington: U.S. Government Printing Office, 1962). *The Quality of Outdoor Recreation: As Evidenced by User Satisfaction,* Report to the Outdoor Recreation Resources Review Commission, Study Report 5 (Washington: U.S. Government Printing Office, 1962).

[22] Nahrum A. Medalia, *Community Perception of Air Quality: An Opinion Survey on Clarkston, Washington,* Environmental Health Series (Cincinnati: U.S. Department of Health, Education, and Welfare, 1965).

[23] *Public Awareness and Concern with Air Pollution in the St. Louis Metropolitan Area,* Public Administration and Metropolitan Affairs Program, Southern Illinois University (Washington: U.S. Department of Health, Education, and Welfare, 1965).

[24] Paul N. Borsky, *Community Reactions to Air Force Noise,* WADD Technical Report 60-689, parts I and II (Dayton: Distributed by U.S. Department of Commerce, Office of Technical Services. 1961).

respondent were faced with a decision in real life.[25] A man who, sitting in his living room, says he would favor a waste treatment plant may behave somewhat differently in a voting booth where the question is posed in terms of authorizing a bond issue, and still differently when the issue is a matter for discussion by a neighborhood group where he is open to new information and to interaction with peers and authorities. There is a lesson in the account of the professor who said he didn't know what he thought of a complex issue because he had not started to talk about it. An election with a yes or no choice lends itself especially to polling prediction and verification. Where the issue is more complex and the range of answers susceptible to wider interpretation, the procedures require supplementing, as was revealed by the forecasts of consumer preference for a paragon of a car called the Edsel. Ideally, the polling should follow after a much more searching investigation in depth which would isolate the factors of environment and personality that may be expected to figure in the final choice.

Although the polling techniques have been popular for a quarter of a century there seems to have been no attempt to find out trends in stated opinion toward the environment during that period. Nor has there been published any successful correlation of opinion survey and content analysis for environmental attitudes at the same place and time.

Akin to the opinion poll, though more concrete in its findings and more provocative in its interpretation, is the examination of actual consumer choices. This is a third avenue of study. The school of thought that argues that the public generally "gets what it wants" asks where people go for recreation in order to find their taste in recreational facilities, and asks what they are willing to pay for water as a measure of the value they place upon it.[26] Such analysis, where its use is practicable, raises basic and disturbing questions for it may well challenge accepted beliefs as to preferences. The trouble here is that so few aspects of environment are subject to free pricing, and that so few past decisions have been made without the encumbrance of extensive social guides which impose constraints and offer incentives. It is much easier to work out shadow prices and comparative valuation of uses for purposes of benefit-cost calculation than it is to trace out the effects of different value judgments along trails of practical choices that are hedged with public prods and carrots. The opportunities to refine estimates of this sort are large

[25] E. J. Baur, "Opinion Change in a Public Controversy," *Public Opinion Quarterly,* 26 (1962), pp. 212–26.

[26] Nathaniel Wollman and others, *The Value of Water in Alternative Uses* (Albuquerque: University of New Mexico Press, 1962), pp. 6–19.

and increasingly recognized. Herfindahl and Kneese point out, for example, that "preferences for pollution-free air can perhaps be inferred from relative land values, expenditures for air purifiers, and commuting costs people are willing to incur to avoid polluted air."[27]

Rather than to ask the citizen what he wants or to deduce his preferences from what he ends up taking, it is possible to look into how he goes about making his choice in daily life. Because the models of decision making are far from satisfactory and because the task of sorting out all of the factors bearing on a decision is intricate at best, this fourth avenue has been pursued only a short distance. Thus far, the studies of organization decision making have given little attention to broad environmental considerations.[28] Geographic studies have tended to focus on perception of particular elements in the environment. Lucas traced out the concepts of wilderness, with its elements of beauty and solitude, as held by users of the Boundary Waters Canoe Area.[29] Situations of distinct hazard from natural phenomena may present problems of perception in a clear light.[30] Kates studied the perception of flood hazard as it related to adoption of loss-reduction measures and, with others, compared fresh-water and coastal situations.[31] Saarinen investigated the perception of drought hazard by Great Plains farmers.[32] Meda White examined the perception of tornado disaster by persons responsible for taking relief measures.[33] The Ohio State Disaster Research Center has

[27] Orris C. Herfindahl and Allen V. Kneese, *Quality of the Environment: An Economic Approach to Some Problems in Using Land, Water and Air* (Washington: Resources for the Future, Inc., 1965), p. 29.

[28] Gore, *loc. cit.* An interesting description of opinion in relation to land and water use organization is given in: Charles K. Warriner, "Public Opinion and Collective Action: Formation of a Watershed District," *Administrative Science Quarterly,* 6 (1961), pp. 333–59. He concludes, "the 'need' arises as the organization comes into being and thus is as much a creator of the need as the need is the creator of the institution" (p. 358).

[29] Robert C. Lucas, "Wilderness Perception and Use: The Example of the Boundary Water Canoe Area," *Natural Resources Journal,* 3 (1964), pp. 394–411.

[30] Ian Burton and Robert W. Kates, "The Perception of Natural Hazards in Resource Management," *Natural Resources Journal,* 3 (1964), pp. 412–41.

[31] Robert W. Kates, *Hazard and Choice Perception in Flood Plain Management* (Chicago: University of Chicago Geography Research Papers, No. 78, 1962).

[32] Thomas Frederick Saarinen, *Perception of the Drought Hazard on the Great Plains* (Chicago: University of Chicago Department of Geography Research Paper No. 106, 1966).

[33] Meda M. White, "Role Conflict in Disasters: A Reconsideration," paper presented at American Sociological Association, 1962. See also Harry Estill Moore, and F. L. Bates, J. P. Alston, M. M. Fuller, M. V. Layman, D. L. Mischer, and M. M. White, *And the Winds Blew* (Austin: Hogg Foundation for Mental Health, 1964).

pursued the problem of how group interaction affects response to a disaster situation.[34]

A fifth and possibly more revealing method of assessing attitudes is found in subjecting people to experimental situations in which they are asked to voice opinions after being exposed to a variety of information and persuasion and to interaction with peers seeking answers to the same problem. In the Chicago study of attitudes toward water, groups of young adults of relatively homogeneous education and age were given the opportunity to learn, discuss, and take positions toward a series of problems involving pollution and other conflictive uses of water. This more nearly approximates an actual decision situation, and makes it possible to observe the effects of changes in experience and in the opinions of their fellows. So far as is known, this is the first venture along that path in assessing attitudes toward environmental quality.

From the scattered evidence accumulated along all five avenues, a few conclusions seem warranted. Generalizations are difficult because there are no adequate models of personality and attitude formation to which to relate the empirical findings.

Perhaps the most obvious observation, as might be deduced from the earlier assertion as to distortion in perception, is that different people may view the same segment of the environment differently. In two neighboring Georgia towns taking water from the same stream, one group of citizens regard the taste as satisfactory, the other as unsatisfac-

[34] Studies published by the National Academy of Sciences–National Research Council, Disaster Research Group (formerly Committee on Disaster Studies), Washington, D.C.: Lewis M. Killian, *A Study of Response to the Houston, Texas, Fireworks Explosion,* Disaster Study No. 2, Publication No. 391, 1956; Anthony F. Wallace, *Tornado in Worcester: An Exploratory Study of Individual and Community Behavior in an Extreme Situation,* Disaster Study No. 3, Publication No. 392, 1956; Fred C. Ikle and Harry V. Kincaid, *Social Aspects of Wartime Evacuation of American Cities, with Particular Emphasis on Long-Term Housing and Re-Employment,* Disaster Study No. 4, Publication No. 393, 1956; George W. Baker and John H. Rohrer (ed.), *Symposium on Human Problems in the Utilization of Fallout Shelters,* Disaster Study No. 12, Publication No. 800, 1960; *Field Studies of Disaster Behavior: An Inventory,* Disaster Study No. 14, Publication No. 886, 1961; Raymond W. Mack and George W. Baker, *The Occasion Instant: The Structure of Social Responses to Unanticipated Air Raid Warnings,* Disaster Study No. 15, Publication No. 945, 1961; George W. Baker (ed.), *Behavioral Science and Civil Defense,* Disaster Study No. 16, Publication No. 997, 1962; F. Bates, *The Social and Psychological Consequences of a Natural Disaster: A Longitudinal Study of Hurricane Audrey,* Disaster Study No. 18, Publication No. 1081, 1963; Harry E. Moore, *Before the Wind; A Study of the Response to Hurricane Carla,* Disaster Study No. 19, Publication No. 1095, 1963.

tory.[35] A landscape which seems friendly and inviting to one traveler is austere and hostile to another.[36] Perceptions of "dirty" water, "ugly" landscapes, "barren wastes," "murky" hazes, do not appear to conform to any universal aesthetic. Without commenting on how these perceptions differ or how their variance is related to other factors, a few other conclusions can be stated.

Judgment as to the severity of a perceived aspect of the environment varies greatly from person to person. Two people in the same metropolitan area may see air pollution as high or low, while agreeing that it constitutes an impairment of the habitat. Two dwellers on the same flood plain may regard flooding as frequent or infrequent, severe or benign.

So also may the city dwellers' concern with environmental quality differ. Even when the degree of severity is seen similarly, their expression of anxiety over its occurrence may vary widely. Thus, their ability to perceive niceties and complexities of the same phenomena of clouded stream or disfigured mesa-top is diverse.

Closely linked with concern is the sense of capacity to change or adjust to the environment. This ranges from the fatalistic acceptance of any feature—pleasurable or obnoxious—to confidence in individual or collective competence to correct the perceived faults. The view of capacity to deal with environment may be expressed in relation to particular aspects of land, water, plants, and air, or it may show in a general attitude toward nature.

The broad value orientations found by Kluckhohn and Strodtbeck in their study of five communities—Mormon, Texan, Spanish-American, Zuni, and Navaho—in the U.S. Southwest seem to apply more widely.[37] Their man-nature classes conform to the commonly held theory that people in their orientation toward nature may be grouped as seeing man in a position of: (1) mastery over nature, (2) subjugation to nature, and (3) harmony with nature. These orientations are seen as related on the one hand to other cultural behavior, motives, and perception of reality, and on the other hand to the social structure and process of groups.

But why are there these great and persistent variations? The circum-

[35] Robert S. Ingolds, "Taste Test Taxes Theories," Engineering Experiment Station, Georgia Institute of Technology, Atlanta, Georgia. Reprint No. 176 from 1964 *Water Works and Wastes Engineering.*
[36] Joseph Sonnenfeld, "Variable Values in Space and Landscape: An Inquiry into the Nature of Environmental Necessity," *Journal of Social Issues,* 22 (in press).
[37] Florence Rockwood Kluckhohn and Fred L. Strodtbeck, *Variations in Value Orientations* (Evanston: Row, Peterson and Company, 1961), pp. 1–48, 363–65.

stances in which attitudes may change or be open to change may offer some clues, although it is unlikely that the variations can ever be wholly accounted for. Ingrained in the mythology of resources management are a number of explanations that apparently do not hold water in contemporary American society. For example, no close relation has been shown between physical setting and attitudes. In the semiarid landscape of the Southwest, the value orientations toward man in relation to nature do not reveal homogeneity with regard to the same landscape: subcultures have different orientations toward the same physical phenomena but there are not absolute differences between distinct cultures; the same components appear in different rank orders.[38] In the recent Chicago studies of attitudes towards water, American young adults do not appear to vary accordingly to the aridity or humidity of the environment in which they spent their earlier years. Neither do their attitudes seem to differ with religious training and membership. If these negative findings are correct, much of the belief popular among government officers that people raised in dry areas have distinctive attitudes toward water in contrast to those raised in the humid East is challenged. The public expression of concern about water may be different in Nevada than northern Maine, but explanation must be sought beyond the physical aspects of childhood environment.

Four sets of factors do appear to play some kind of part in attitude formation: the decision situation, the individual's experience with the environment, his perception of his role, and his competence in dealing with its complexity. A different classification of the factors no doubt could be more systematic but these groupings are convenient.

Perhaps the most careful studies of the circumstances of public choice of environmental quality have centered upon the issue of whether or not public water supplies should be fluoridated and on the social situations in which public action is taken. The decision to fluoridate as a measure against tooth decay often appears as a single question for popular or council vote. Studies made of a few of the communities in which it has been proposed and adopted or rejected since 1944 throw light on the generality of knowledge as to attitude formation.[39] Paul, Gamson,

[38] Kluckhohn and Strodtbeck, *op. cit.,* pp. 341–42.
[39] Benjamin D. Paul, William A. Gamson, and S. Stephen Kegeles (editors), *Trigger for Community Conflict: The Case of Fluoridation* (eight articles), *Journal of Social Issues,* 17 (1961), No. 4, pp. 1–81, quotation on page 7. See also: Fluoridation (special issue of 22 articles), *Journal of the American Dental Association,* 65 (1962), pp. 578–717; Robert M. O'Shea and S. Stephen Kegeles, "An Analysis of Anti-Fluoridation Letters," *Journal of Health and Human Behavior,* 4 (1963), pp. 135–40; Arnold Simmel and David B. Ast, "Some Correlates of Opinion on Fluoridation," *American Journal of Public Health,* 52 (1962), pp. 1269–73.

and Kegeles, in reviewing what is now a large literature of social studies, point out that people who feel deprived or alienated by society tend to express resentment by voting against fluoridation, and that the local leaders of opposition are moved by feelings of the "remoteness and impersonality of the sources of power and influence affecting the daily life of the individual." When the histories of fluoridation campaigns are examined, it is observed that the same action which would be advantageous at one stage may set back the effort at another stage, and that often the leaders of campaigns, some of them professionals, may work against their own purposes because of their inability to recognize the roles expected of them. Although there has been considerable analysis of demographic, educational, and economic characteristics of voters and leaders, the more critical points for further investigation seem to center on personality traits and on the local social and political situation in which the decision is made.

Few issues offering choice of environmental quality have been investigated in as much detail as the fluoridation disputes. The aims are less clear and the range of possible means is much wider when an ordinance to ban billboards is up for a vote, or when the farmers' use of pesticides is at stake. Less is known about effects which the circumstances of social organization and personal interaction may have. In an interesting review of studies of why American farmers have been slow to accept recommended soil conservation practices, Held and Clawson examine the scattered evidence on farmers' attitudes toward erosion control measures and find that while certain factors, such as reluctance to change old methods and age of operator, may be significant they should be examined in the context of the tenure, farm management, and cost-price relations in which the farmer acts.[40] The parts played by perception of soil conditions and by personality have received only passing attention.

Probably the greater part of studies to date have dealt with the intricate set of relations involved in human response to environmental stimuli. An excellent sampling of representative work is given by Kates and Wohlwill in a recent issue of the *Journal of Social Issues*.[41] They note the paucity of psychological study of the effects of physical environment on man's behavior, and call attention especially to its significance for the professions that design new rural or urban environments.

[40] R. Burnell Held and Marion Clawson, *Soil Conservation in Perspective* (Baltimore: The Johns Hopkins Press for Resources for the Future, 1965), pp. 254–62.
[41] Robert W. Kates and J. F. Wohlwill (eds.), "Man's Response to the Physical Environment," *Journal of Social Issues*, 22 (in press).

At the most elementary level, it was shown that in the two Georgia towns noted above the town which found its water taste unsatisfactory received water from time to time from an alternate source having less pronounced taste, whereas the town regarding the taste as satisfactory drew only on what the other branded an obnoxious source. Experience counts, but does not have a simple linear relation to either perception of the environment or willingness to deal with it. Thus, Kates finds, flood plain dwellers with direct exposure to floods have different perceptions of the hazard and a greater propensity to cope with it. Lucas shows that the canoeist views the same wilderness differently than does the motor-boater, and that the responsible government officials have perceptions conforming to neither. Saarinen demonstrates that wheat farmers on the Central Great Plains become more sensitive to drought hazard up to late middle age, and that then their awareness declines sharply. People who are more annoyed by noisy aircraft tend to be those who fear air crashes, who are less convinced of the importance of the air base to the area's welfare, and who are also annoyed by automobile noise. Only a few cross-cultural comparisons have been made. Each such finding throws light on the wisdom of public measures to manage an aspect of environment by sharpening the understanding of how individual citizens and officials view the same physical landscape.

If a major aspect of the individual's perception of the world around him is related to his sense of his own role in that world, then it becomes important to seek out his identification of himself. Oftentimes students of environmental problems like to categorize themselves and others as behaving according to a professional stereotype. The economist optimizes net returns, the engineer gets the right things built, and the conservationist stops the *wrong* things from being built. There are niceties and colorful elaborations that need not be repeated. Just how much the individual's identification by training, professional status, and interaction with his peers leads him to behave in particular ways toward his environment has not been demonstrated. By analogy with other professions, such as medicine,[42] it might be expected that the sense of vocational role would be strong and that it would be reinforced by a high degree of self selection among students who, sharing certain stereotypes, choose a profession that they hope will be congenial.

A fundamental line of inquiry is followed by Strodtbeck and his associates in examining sex identification. Because it has relevance both to the individual's view of the world around him and to his sense of role

---

[42] Everett C. Hughes, *Student's Culture and Perspectives* (Lawrence: University of Kansas School of Law, 1961).

in interaction with other people, sex identity may be a powerful means of recognizing personality traits that are significant in formation of attitudes toward environment. In the study of attitudes toward water, it was found that young American men when confronted with situations in which water problems were presented as either severe or not severe, and in which the possibility of taking positive action was seen as either promising or not promising, responded very differently according to the sex role with which they consciously and unconsciously identified themselves. Thus, the man who was both consciously and unconsciously strong in male characteristics was more likely to take action if he was told the problem was capable of solution, whereas the one with strong identification of himself as having female characteristics had the greater propensity to act when the problem was not likely of solution. Other findings are given in the report already noted. The point here is that role identification may turn out to be a highly significant factor in attitude formation.

The fourth set of factors may be grouped under the heading of what Henry and Schlien call "affective complexity."[43] This refers to the personality attributes that permit an individual to be aware of complexity in the world around him, and to respond to them without being entirely defensive or threatened. It implies openness to impressions from the outside and ability to confidently incorporate them in guiding his own behavior.

Although no studies have been made of this set of attributes as they relate to natural resource uses, the approach seems worth noting as aiming at situations that often attach to management of the environment. Quality decisions always refer to environmental change, to individual preferences for change, to a complex environment, and to programs with ambiguous aims. Much of the effort to change the urban scene presumes the response of persons who, finding the new city in conflict with the value orientation of their culture and the preferences cultivated by past experience, have the personality attributes to be able to explore modifications of both the city and their own behavior without merely launching war upon the city.

The scholar who predicts what future preferences the public will express for the quality of water or air, and the administrator who wonders how far a later constituency may tolerate a current decision as to standards, may ask how likely are the underlying attitudes, once

[43] William E. Henry and John M. Schlien, "Affective Complexity and Psychotherapy: Some Comparisons of Time-Limited and Unlimited Treatment," *Journal of Projective Techniques,* 22 (1958), pp. 153–62.

tagged, to change. Also, judging from the number of students of resource management who appear to feel that what the people should
prefer coincides with what they themselves prefer, there are some who
brood over how they can manipulate public attitudes in what they regard
as the right direction. Indeed, a considerable part of the public information expenditures of the federal and state departments dealing with
natural resources is based on conviction that a flow of facts about resources and their use will influence public action either by changing
attitudes or by providing information on which people can act more
intelligently. The Chicago study on attitudes toward water finds pronounced differences among managerial groups in their belief in the
degree to which their actions can modify public attitudes.

Insofar as the attitudes are related to role identification and affective
complexity they may be regarded as largely inflexible. The decision
situation—the time of the vote, the leaders who force the decision, the
way they phrase the question—is much more subject to alteration.
Among the numerous aspects of environmental stimulation, probably
the one most susceptible to change is the information about environmental conditions and ways of managing them. Although certain findings
suggest that the information alone, as in the case of a flood hazard map
or a government pamphlet about wind erosion, may have little effect
upon attitudes toward those phenomena, other studies indicate that if
the situation in which choice is exercised is modified or if the individual's
sense of efficacy in dealing with the confusion of the world is changed
suitably, the information takes on different significance. Given favorable
circumstances (and this qualification may be crucial) there is no reason
to think that some amount of shift in attitude would not follow the
receipt of new information about the environment.[44] Just how far the
shift will go, and just how much personality traits, such as role identification, will have to do with it, is far from clear.

The most difficult question remaining is whether a shift in attitude
would have any perceptible effect upon the decisions reached about
environmental quality. Experimental evidence seems wholly lacking,
and most of the observations of a curbstone character are made without
a rigorous scheme of analysis. Generalizations must come from definition or from casual reflection on a few past decisions.

One striking fact is that a large number of environmental quality
decisions are made by people who feel a strong professional identifica-

[44] For a review of changes in attitudes toward culture groups, see E. E. Davis,
Attitude Change: A Review and Bibliography of Selected Research, Social Science
Clearing House Documents, No. 19 (Paris: UNESCO, 1965).

tion. Their view of themselves as conservationists, economists, sanitary engineers, foresters, etc., may be expected to shape their perception of the environment and their competence to handle it. In these roles they not only inherit customary ways of defining significant parts of the environment but they are disposed to distort or ignore phenomena that they regard as beyond their professional responsibility or competence. (If you can't measure a diseconomy, sweep it under the rug.) Their perceptions and preferences become the implicit and usually unchallenged determinants of plans presented for public choice.

A second fact is that these professional judgments often involve assessment of public preferences that go largely unchecked. An engineer's view of public valuation of a polluted stream or a soot-ridden sky rarely is tested by investigation and commonly enters into public decision in situations in which individual citizens can express a disapproval of the plan but not of its assumptions as to their preferences. When the New York Board of Water Supply decided against using Hudson River sources it had no generalized scientific evidence on the way in which citizens of those cultural groups regard water sources, it lacked any findings on New York preferences, and it passed on its judgment in a form which eliminated any public expression of those preferences: since it was concluded without verification that the people wanted upland sources, they were asked to vote for upland sources as the best solution. Their favorable vote could neither confirm nor deny the conclusion.

In the absence of a more adequate model of decision making, the testing of the influence of attitudes on both officials and the related citizen groups remains largely conjectural. It may be useful, nevertheless, to outline two hypotheses that grow out of experience with water resource management debates and that do not appear to be inconsistent with observed relationships. These indicate the kind of question calling for systematic examination, and are selected from more than twenty appearing in the report of the Chicago study.

1. Because of the complexity of systems of water management, the ambiguity of their ownership, and ignorance of the natural processes explaining their behavior, there is a strong tendency to rely upon exterior authority for judgment as to management of water quality. In simple decision networks, where individual control of environment is large, the unknown is explained by myth: in complex networks the judgment is referred to professional experts.

2. Perception of the effects of water management upon others is a function of the degree to which the individual regards man as a master of nature and to which he resents manipulation of himself by others.

In each case the disposition to take public action is seen as related to the personality traits of the individuals involved. How much these are confined or magnified by the social setting in which the decision is reached is difficult to say.

Until recent years a high proportion of public decisions on resource management in the United States were taken following great natural disasters or in anticipation of serious human deprivation. Flood control legislation often followed in the muddy wake of major floods, and soil conservation measures sprang up in the lengthened shadow of dust clouds. Timber management was promoted in part by the anticipation of a future timber shortage. Much of the rhetoric hinged on the fear of a reported crisis or of a new one looming in the years ahead. Such appeals are still strong, as with the brooding concern for the human effects of pesticides and fungicides and with the dark prediction of national water shortage. However, the rising level of per capita production and the accelerating pace of technologic change enlarges the conditions of choice in the direction of greater freedom. As shown by a recent report by the Committee on Water of the National Academy of Sciences,[45] the unfolding opportunities for water management are in exploring the whole range of possible alternatives in transactions with the environment, and in weighing their relative social impacts.

This is a turn away from the customary promotion of single solutions in an atmosphere of present or impending crisis. Consideration of alternatives for changing the environment implies less reliance on choices by a technical elite and more confidence in a base of citizens who have the maturity to deal with complex and probabilistic conditions. To the extent such a shift occurs, sensitivity to the direction of public attitudes, as well as to their limitations, may be expected to take on greater importance.

Faced with trying to understand public decisions on a stinking stream and a scarred landscape such as those presented to Boulder's voters, social science can offer a few sturdy methods and a larger set of questions that remain unanswered. By content analysis it is possible to define the issues and the attitudes toward them as articulated in the public argument. By opinion survey of a representative sample of the population, the expressed attitudes of sectors of the electorate can be assessed, and a prediction of voters' behavior can be checked against the vote itself. By analysis of the voting situation a rough judgment can be

[45] "Alternatives in Water Management," National Academy of Sciences Research Report No. 1408, August 1966 (Washington, National Academy of Sciences–National Research Council).

reached on the extent to which conflicts or compacts among public officials and political groups in the community may so operate as to obscure any voter preference as to the kind of environment the people prefer. There are slight but provocative grounds for expecting that the stated attitudes would vary in some degree with length and type of the respondents' experience with stream and mesa, that perception of severity would vary with social status, and that propensity to act would be related to role identification and affective complexity. These and other data provide an initial base from which to speculate on the situations in which various types of information might promote changes in attitudes if given to the public at the appropriate time.

Because there are no satisfactory models of the decision process or of the interaction of factors affecting attitude formation, the speculation for Boulder or any other community could, at best, only explore pragmatic relations or tentative theory. Basic research is needed on decision processes and attitude formation, particularly in settings where resource management produces nonvendible benefits. The network of decisions should be described in sufficient detail to permit recognition of power relations among individuals and groups. The typology of attitudes toward environment invites much more precise analysis. These attitudes deserve searching examination in experimental conditions where the personality traits of the subjects are known and where the inputs of information and the decision situation are partly controlled. From those investigations may be expected increased understanding of human response which would permit a more incisive wording of questions for opinion surveys and, in turn, more intelligent interpretation of their results. An auxiliary step would be thoughtful appraisal of environmental quality features of opinion surveys of the past twenty-five years in order to recover data that has been lost from sight.

As these studies proceed they will throw light on how decisions in truth are made, on how the professional's own preferences figure in the proposed solutions, on what he thinks the citizen prefers, on what the citizen, given a genuine choice, does prefer, and on how all of these may shift with the circumstances and experience surrounding the choice. In a time when many types of environmental change are little suited to precise definition or quantitative expression, when there are few market checks of value judgments, and when professional judgment obscures assumptions as to preferences, the future public management of the environment's human satisfactions has growing need for discovery of the delicate process by which individual preferences find their way into public choices of vista, taste, odor, and sound.

David Lowenthal

ASSUMPTIONS BEHIND THE PUBLIC ATTITUDES

Gilbert White's paper is comprehensive in scope, empirical in structure, and rational in outlook. My comments will focus mainly on an aspect of environmental problems antecedent to those he has dealt with —that is, the nature and significance of assumptions that underlie attitudes toward the environment. But first let me comment on a few specific points raised in the paper itself.

To Mr. White's cogent warnings about the pitfalls in the way of finding out what people really think of environment and of how thought relates to action, I would append some additional caveats:

Inarticulateness. On a tour of Hearst's castle at San Simeon not long ago, a lady in my group expressed lively and spontaneous delight when we reached Hearst's private library, a well-furnished, vaguely Gothic room. "Oh, this is beautiful," she exclaimed. On the way out I asked what it was she particularly liked. "I don't know," she said, "I just *liked* it." Was it the shape of the room, its contents, the style, the color? She could not tell me; it just made her "feel good" to be in it. This experience is, alas, typical of many of my attempts to elicit environmental preferences. The problem is, I think, that most people are unfamiliar

David Lowenthal, *research associate with the American Geographical Society, is currently also a Guggenheim Fellow engaged in a study of past and present attitudes toward nature and landscape. He taught geography at Vassar College from 1952 to 1956 and was a Fulbright Research Fellow at the University of the West Indies, Jamaica, during 1956–57. He is the author of a biography of George Perkins Marsh and editor of a new edition of Marsh's* Man and Nature. *Mr. Lowenthal is also editor of* Environmental Perception and Behavior, *being brought out in the University of Chicago Department of Geography Research Paper series, and author of many journal articles. He was born in New York City in 1923 and received his B.S. from Harvard, his M.A. in geography from the University of California, and his Ph.D. in history from the University of Wisconsin.*

with such issues—indeed, with *most* environmental experiences. "You cannot see things till you know roughly what they are," C. S. Lewis has pointed out;[1] and you cannot express lucid opinions about things until you have experienced them. Many personal preferences are inchoate, diffuse, irrational, and can hardly be formulated concretely even to ourselves. Views about the environment are not the only ones that are difficult to communicate, but many are of this nature. That is why attitudes are often explicitly stated only *after* an environmental decision has been acted on—a decision that significantly changes the world people live in and forces them to take conscious note of the milieu.

Impropriety. Some people feel that it is not only difficult to analyze their environmental preferences but somehow inappropriate, even wrong, to do so. Like a work of art the environment, whether natural or man-made, is popularly considered beyond the scope of normative judgments. "I don't think one should analyze the principles of design—you just *feel* them," a Seattle interior designer maintained recently;[2] no doubt his clients would concur. Just as many people consider religion a matter of faith not open to argument, so do they consider environmental preferences to be purely personal and not to be subject to (and hence diminished or changed by) public or scientific scrutiny.

The impact of crises. As Mr. White has indicated, subjective concerns profoundly alter environmental choices. People involved in actual or threatened change may rapidly learn a great deal about the capabilities and limitations of the environment, but all they learn is apt to be overwhelmed, distorted, and negated by feeling. A new understanding of traffic patterns and land values along an expressway route will weigh little in the balance to a householder who has just undergone the vivid experience of erecting barricades along a concrete roadway or defending trees from bulldozers—perhaps his first tactile contact with trees since childhood. Similarly, the farmer whose lowland acres will be flooded by a big dam has a totally different impression of the appearance and meaning of such a structure than the tourist at Boulder Dam.

Variability of experience. Environmental views and choices are often fleeting and evanescent, creatures of mood and of moment. A man's feelings about space and traffic, smog and flood control, will differ in rain and shine, peace and war, and according to whether his stomach is empty or full, or maybe overfull. Easier to analyze are differences in viewpoint that depend on season and on daily schedule. At home, on the journey to work, and at business, trees and power lines and water

---

[1] C. S. Lewis, *Out of the Silent Planet* (New York: Collier Books, 1962), p. 42.
[2] Allen Vance Salsbury, quoted in "The Unique World of Interior Design," *Seattle Magazine,* Vol. 3, No. 23 (February 1966), p. 34.

purity look different and assume different priorities; the man who feels entitled to smogless sylvan peace at home may not expect it elsewhere. Some take positive delight in the contrast between beauty and squalor, and find home joys enhanced by commuting perils. "The restfulness of a peaceful countryside" is enhanced, Flint maintains, "at the end of a day of struggle and conflict. . . . It is wonderful after an hour of fighting the most aggressive traffic that the world has ever seen to be able to lean back at home and say 'Boy, it's nice here. We must protect this opportunity.' "[3]

Variability of attentiveness. We all engage in a whole range of environmental perception from conscious attention to detail to diffuse awareness of our entire surroundings. Focused attention is not more objective or informative than generalized impressions; indeed, as Gibson notes, "Everyday perception tends to be selective, creative, fleeting, inexact, generalized, stereotyped," just because imprecise, partly erroneous impressions about the world in general often convey more than exact details about some small segment of it.[4] Both are essential; the driver must remain aware of side-street activity while focusing on the road ahead. Resource managers should bear in mind that public attitudes are based on blurred and holistic as well as on sharp and dissected images of environment.

Interpreting historical evidence. On the other side of the ledger, I have more confidence than Mr. White in the validity of the historical record. Nineteenth-century schoolbooks, in the work he cites, exhibit a consistent and moralistic preference for rural over urban life.[5] "Did McGuffey," Mr. White asks, "speak for the tillers of soil in Indiana?" The answer is a qualified yes. What proportion of Hoosier farmers would have taken this line in a public opinion poll we do not know; but almost all of them were exposed to it in their schooling. McGuffey's and similar texts were more widely disseminated than any other book save the Bible. The opinions they expressed did not always conform to views actually held by the public. (I am reminded of Laurence Wylie's discussion of how French children were taught in school that shooting small birds was

[3] Thomas Flint, comment on paper by William H. Whyte, in A. J. W. Scheffey, ed., *Resources, the Metropolis, and the Land-Grant University,* Cooperative Extension Service, College of Agriculture, University of Massachusetts, Publication 410 (1963), p. 28.

[4] James J. Gibson, *The Perception of the Visual World* (Boston: Houghton Mifflin, 1950), p. 10; George A. Miller, "The Magical Number Seven, Plus or Minus Two: Some Limits on Our Capacity for Processing Information," *Psychological Review,* Vol. 63 (1956), pp. 88–89.

[5] Ruth Miller Elson, *Guardians of Tradition: American Schoolbooks of the Nineteenth Century* (Lincoln: University of Nebraska Press, 1964), pp. 25–28.

wrong, and then came home and bagged them with complete parental sanction.)[6] Nevertheless, textbooks were significant in forming nineteenth-century American attitudes. The dicta they expressed were *normative*—they were acceptable to school boards and to publishers as in line with public morality and the common weal. And the fact that schoolbook views of nature and of man's role in nature were fairly constant throughout the century indicates that these views remained acceptable as ideals to parents who had themselves been indoctrinated. Had they been inconsistent with later experience, such attitudes would have been revised or eliminated from the school texts.

Landscape paintings may likewise yield evidence of public attitudes toward environment. Works of art are not, like textbooks, expressions of normative views; but they are heightened intuitions of what others sense less strongly or explicitly. All art reflects the culture in which it is created, and most of it is a direct response to public taste—men paint pictures that people will buy. Painters of the Hudson River School in the early nineteenth century and later portrayers of the West like Moran and Bierstadt used a panoramic technique with a shifting vanishing point—a real innovation in style. Their work reflected public perception of the American scene as enormous and remote, not to be taken in at a single glance but only by sweeping the horizon. The size and structure of these panoramic views conveyed the vast extent of the country, emphasized its horizontality, and transmitted a feeling of being on a frontier, of looking with the artist into the wilderness. The ultimate in American panoramic painting was the diorama, a strip of canvas on a cylinder unwound behind a stage on which actors performed. The moving panorama was as popular in the nineteenth century as the movies later became. The Mississippi River especially lent itself to panoramic sequences, inspiring dioramas allegedly up to three miles long.[7]

To interpret textbook data and works of art for evidence of public attitudes toward environment is, to be sure, a highly intuitive and subjective process; but most historical understanding is derived in just this way. In the last analysis, the test of validity lies as much in the consistency and the explanatory power of the evidence as in its completeness. All interpretations of the environment are subjective; even professional consensus includes much that is beyond the realm of scientific validation. Purely scientific descriptions of the environment convey little

[6] Laurence Wylie, *Village in the Vaucluse* (Cambridge: Harvard University Press, 1957).

[7] Wolfgang Born, *American Landscape Painting: An Interpretation* (New Haven: Yale University Press, 1948), pp. 75–117.

to most people because verisimilitude requires empathy as well as accuracy.

Ecology and environmental preference. An anthropocentric approach to environment is unavoidable, but one of Mr. White's cautionary remarks seems to me to go beyond the bounds of objective safety. He tells us that "the proper test is not the landscape itself but the response of whoever is stimulated by it." Thus power lines and pylons and highway billboards may offend and repel the viewer, but their ecological impact on the environment is minimal. The distinction is clear, but the priority is dubious. There are environments which please some only at the cost of deprivation, real or fancied, to others—African wildlife preservation is a case in point, where the ecological values of preservationists can be justified locally only by inventing a benefit-cost analysis proving that wild species contribute more to the Gross National Product than domestic animals would.

There are more serious impediments to using pure response as a measuring rod. Some people delight in landscapes which are so physically unstable or biologically unviable that they can be maintained—if at all—only by pumping in human and natural resources at great cost: examples are golf courses, Niagara Falls, the Great Stone Face in New Hampshire, and the Douglas Fir forest, a successional form that will not reproduce itself except on a bared site. If such tastes as these are indulged without regard to ecological health, the environmental fabric may deteriorate so much as to deprive succeeding generations of any good range of opportunity. To ignore ecological quality as a factor in environmental choice is to write off the future. Which of us does not care about the world our children will inhabit? A final objection: one need not subscribe to Aldo Leopold's land ethic to differentiate between the ecologist's and the mathematician's delight in perfection. The mathematician takes pleasure in pure discovery, the ecologist is to some extent morally committed to the sanctity of life or at least to avoiding needless destruction.

I now turn to the heart of the subject considered here—attitudes about environmental decisions. To begin with, why *assess* public opinion? Beyond an abstract desire to know how choices are felt, and a commitment to democratic procedures in a free society, let us consider the following range of reasons for taking the public pulse.

To reach actual decisions. Even when not required to do so by law, resource managers may sometimes genuinely wish to give people what they say they want—that is, to preserve or alter aspects of the environment in conformity with expressed public wishes.

To smooth managerial paths. Whether or not they intend to follow the public voice, decision makers may want to make themselves aware of consumer reactions in advance. Those who know public opinion are likely to be more flexible, less autocratic. Moreover, testing public views gives an impression of willingness to cater to those views and helps to implement decisions. To be persuasive, the environmental manager like any other salesman must keep intimately informed about the preferences and prejudices of his clients.

To alter public opinion. Answering questions is a form of experience, a type of education. Before their views are assessed, people may be quite unaware of an issue or know of it only from vague and misinformed rumor. Opinion polling offers a chance to make the public better informed, more concerned, and more articulate; it may even alter preferences.

These considerations may motivate opinion-taking in any society. But there are few societies in which public participation and the desirability of general education are so widely taken for granted as in the United States. In England last summer I was discussing with an architect-planner the problem assigned him to locate a new town in one of the southern counties. After he outlined some considerations that weighed with his team—distance from existing urban centers, employment opportunities, transportation networks and demands, ecological site characteristics—I asked if he had ascertained *public* preferences about where the town should or should not be built. "Oh, yes," he replied at once, "Sylvia Crowe [a well-known landscape architect] has told us what she thinks on several occasions." For him "the public" meant the informed opinion of experts; people at large could be expected to accept what planners thought was good for them. The Central Electricity Generating Board and some other agencies maintain better public liaison, as Ralph Turvey has assured us in Chapter 3; but many environmental managers in England perceive a deep gulf between themselves as custodians and those whom they serve.[8]

Elitist leadership of this type, however, runs counter to the whole bent of American endeavor; we have traditionally exalted the role and viewpoint of the amateur. We have, in Mr. White's terms, "confidence in a base of citizens who have the maturity to deal with complex and probabilistic conditions."

Officials and other resource managers in fact often share most of the

[8] David Lowenthal and Hugh C. Prince, "The English Landscape," *Geographical Review,* Vol. 54 (1964), pp. 325–29.

public's implicit concepts about man's relations with nature. Examine, for example, the statements quoted by Mr. White from the Department of Interior Yearbook:[9]

"There is dawning in man an understanding of the intertwined cause and effect pattern which makes him subject . . . to every slightest tampering with his total environment." This is a statement not of knowledge but of faith—faith that ecological principles will govern public opinion. Behind this lies an assumption that people can be more rational if they wish, and that the role of reason in public affairs will therefore expand.

"He must be willing to work for quality everywhere, not just in his own back yard." This assumes that Americans can be persuaded to be less selfish and parochial, more able and willing to consider the well-being of all mankind.

"He must wonder not just where his next drink of water is coming from, but what is being done to keep the world's taps from going dry." This is not only a Malthusian view, but implies that water is a nonrenewable resource. The theme of scarcity interrelates, of course, with that of worldwide concern.

Finally let me quote from William O. Douglas's recent book, not official dogma but close enough to it: "A conservation part is not a playground. It is not an amusement center. . . . The conservation park should return man to the environment from which he came."[10] Nature at its "best" or most pure should be revered, not made the locus of pleasure.

These views taken together reflect our faith that we can conquer nature, along with doubt about the moral and aesthetic desirability of doing so; our belief in progress, along with a foreboding that resources are exhaustible and the era of expansion over; and our characteristic tendency to suppose that our highest ideals can become our constant and consistent behavior, given proper leadership.

Such statements disclose the generalizing assumptions of public leaders as well as of the public—assumptions highly significant in forming attitudes about the environment and structuring activity in it. Let me pose a few questions that might stem from the value orientations outlined by Gilbert White.

[9] *Quest for Quality*: U.S. Department of the Interior Conservation Yearbook (Washington: U.S. Government Printing Office, 1965), p. 13.
[10] William O. Douglas, *A Wilderness Bill of Rights* (Boston: Little, Brown and Co., 1965), p. 156.

• What views are held about the impact of environment on man? To what extent do Americans remain naively deterministic in forms of speech, while eschewing environmental determinism in action? How does this ambivalence affect our dealings with the landscape?

• What views are held about man's impact on the environment? Has the conservation movement basically altered laissez-faire attitudes, or is concern about the waste of resources and the mistreatment of nature only a minority veneer over majority neglect? Who is concerned about the irreversible consequences of changing the environment, and why?

• To what extent do people regard nature as part of the moral order? How far is man's treatment of nature condoned, or condemned, on ethical grounds; how much is moral exhortation used to support ecological or economic choices? Wilderness pilgrimages are sometimes seen as redemptive journeys into innocence and aboriginal virtue; American fiction, art, and nature writing are full of this theme.[11] But millions mostly prefer intensely gregarious and comfortable outdoor activity, camping faucet to faucet with laundromat and bridge partners close at hand. The call of the wild is satisfied vicariously, by throwing symbolic water on a campfire as the park ranger turns off the gas jet; how many want *more* than this?

• How are desirable, precious, or life-enhancing aspects of the environment generally categorized? Do most people separate "historic" from "scenic" vistas, and think of the latter as "natural"? It would be useful to compare American classifications with the exemplary list recently devised by a study group of the British "Countryside in 1970" conference. Among "Natural Treasures," for example, they distinguish (1) Natural reserves, (2) Geological features such as faults and folds and typical rock formations, (3) Physiographical phenomena such as types of erosion and deposition, (4) Ecological site types, (5) Biological features such as the habitats of rare animals and plants, and (6) Eight different types of scenic features: areas, views, vantage points, prominent features, skylines, "effective groups of lesser features," river and other water attractions, and woodland and trees.[12] Do Americans make as many distinctions, and are they of the same mixed nature? When do we conceive aspects of environment in terms of location, when in terms of physical feature, of ecological situation, of use?

And finally, two issues earlier touched on:

[11] See Leo Marx, *The Machine and the Garden: Technology and the Pastoral Ideal in America* (New York: Oxford University Press, 1964).

[12] *Preservation of Natural, Historic and Other Treasures,* Report of Study Group No. 8, "The Countryside in 1970," Second Conference, London 10–12 November 1965. London: The Royal Society of Arts and The Nature Conservancy, p. 18.

• How far is interest in environmental quality today subordinated to hopes and plans for the future? How much that is ugly and shapeless do we ignore or condone in order to realize a dream? I recently visited the Santa Barbara campus of the University of California, set in a vast no-man's land several miles north of the city. Emerging from the freeway, you are stopped at a small shed in the midst of nowhere. "That will be 25 cents, please," says the guard. "What for?" you ask. "For parking on the campus." "Where is the campus?" "You're on it," he says, gesturing in front of you; off in the middle distance you can just make out a few structures set in a wilderness of sand and rubble. And he hands you a campus map which shows the location of the *future* University buildings.

"The Americans *love* their country, not, indeed, *as it is,*" wrote a German traveler in the 1830's, "but *as it will be.*"[13] The futurist strain remains as powerful today, to judge from a contemporary encomium on Washington. What is beautiful about the city, it is claimed, is its plans for the future—"a massive redesign of Pennsylvania Avenue which . . . would give Washington a magnificent vista . . . such as L'Enfant envisioned when he planned the city 174 years ago"[14]; a Potomac that "President Johnson has pledged that one day . . . will be sufficiently free of pollution for swimming." Washington is said to be emblematic of cities that ask, "What shall we leave to the age that comes after ours?"[15] Our own age is forgotten in the excitement of envisioned Progress. Disneyland, the country of our consensual imagination, comprises Frontierland, Adventureland, Tomorrowland, Fantasyland, and a turn-of-the-century Main Street; the present has no place in it.

• To what extent is environmental quality regarded as an integral part of life, rather than a separate package of goods? Just as we zone space, so we compartmentalize time. I referred above to the commuter who enjoyed stress. There are few moments of the day in which a concern for environmental quality is uppermost; there are few days in the year when we are deliberately concerned with the nature of the milieu. The rest of the time we pretty well ignore it. Exposure to environmental stimuli is a conscious, even a *self*-conscious act, highly limited in diurnal and calendar time, in duration, and above all in location.

Consider the Mt. Rainier syndrome in Seattle. Everyone is highly conscious of the Cascade range and constantly refers to it. You often hear "Well, it's out today!" and that means just one thing; Rainier can be seen on the skyline. But Seattle also has an avenue named Rainier,

---

[13] Francis J. Grund, *The Americans in Their Moral, Social, and Political Relations* (London: 1837), II, 263–64.

[14] Russell Scearce, "The First City," *Mainliner*, Vol. 10, No. 3 (March 1966).

[15] Michael Frome in *Mainliner*, Vol. 10, No. 3 (March 1966).

intended to focus on the mountain as a vista. Rainier Avenue is a tawdry mess of "eye-scratching utility poles and wires, miserable street lighting, carelessly hung traffic signals . . . and a cacophony of poorly designed buildings" and billboards. "The ultimate symbol of nature in the Northwest, Mt. Rainier," an architectural critic concludes, "is desecrated by what man hath wrought. . . . This avenue stands as a sorry . . . monument to our carelessness, indifference and lack of interest in our environment."[16] Why is this so? The reason is clear; like most of us, Seattleites find environment beauty at a *distance* sufficient; they do not object to the mess nearby because enjoyment and beauty are taken for granted as remote and occasional attributes, not as everyday pleasures or a part of ordinary life. They focus attention on nature far away, and enjoy it on weekends and vacations. Appropriately enough, the main attraction of the World's Fair Space Needle in Seattle's City Center is the view *away* from it.

When smog or effluents render environments obtrusively unpleasant, people take action; but visual blight leaves them mostly unmoved. Environmental quality as a positive feature of everyday life is regarded— even by some advocates—as a matter for aesthetes and zealots. Thus Washington's national arts center is said to be meant "to emphasize America's interest in the aesthetics"—obviously a side interest. "*Beauty* . . . makes Washington a city of which Americans can be *proud*," runs a blurb. "What makes it a city they can *enjoy* is the endless variety of *entertainment*. . . ."[17] Note the distinction; one does not *enjoy* beauty, it is just a part of the image. Some planners too think beauty comes in standard bits, a plaza, a fountain, a row of trees, a shopping mall, added in wherever there is space, regardless of location and site, just as preservers of old houses remove them to new locations out of all historical and geographical context. We all tend, in Kenneth Boulding's term, to be cheerful polluters, ready to heed the exhortation on a Fresno billboard: "Help Beautify Our Junkyards—Throw Away Something Lovely Today."

An ingrained dualism impels us to dichotomize, polarize, and compartmentalize experience. Both man and landscape are viewed as simple functions: man as though at any particular time he does either one thing *or* another, landscapes as though they existed for one purpose *or* another. As long as landscapes are considered either ideal *or* hopeless, as long as decisions involving environmental quality are seen in terms of polar opposites, little progress can be made either in changing public views or in improving the livability of our milieu.

16 Victor Steinbrueck, "Here's Garbage In Your Eye!," *Seattle Post-Intelligencer, Northwest Today*, February 27, 1966, p. 11.
17 Russell Scearce, *op. cit.* [italics mine].

Chapter Six

NEEDED IMPROVEMENTS IN POLICIES AND INSTITUTIONS

Norton E. Long

⌠ NEW TASKS FOR ALL LEVELS ⌡
⌡ OF GOVERNMENT ⌠

The subject of environmental quality ranges from the health hazards of water and air pollution to the eyesores of billboards and junk yards. Accordingly, agreement on what constitutes quality varies from subject to subject. Indeed what constitutes hazard is a matter not only of dispute among laymen but even among the experts. Despite the impressive statistical evidence, even the experts still exhibit significant disagreement about the effects of smoking. The improvement of environmental quality requires, as at least an initial condition, some sufficient concern on the part of important elements of the public with its present and likely future condition. The highly individualistic, every-man-for-himself, ideology has only recently given way to belated recognition of its practical impossibility in an increasingly crowded urban environment.

Present governmental structure reflects a past whose problems could be dealt with in limited areas and with limited resources. The problems of environmental quality, except where approaching the catastrophic, are poorly recognized in the conventional wisdom and are ill adapted to receive appropriate recognition through the existing structure of government, especially at state and local levels. A glance at the appropriations and staffing for air pollution control at state and local levels outside of California indicates that whatever the objective facts, public recognition and appreciation is a needed precondition for governmental action.

We are today in the process of changing the governmental structure

Norton E. Long, *professor of American Community Government at Brandeis University, is also associated with the Massachusetts Institute of Technology—Harvard University Center for Urban Studies. In addition to university teaching at Western Reserve, Northwestern, and Michigan, he held executive positions in the Office of Price Administration and the National Housing Administration in the 1940's and was staff consultant to the Governor of Illinois from 1961 to 1963. He is author of* The Polity, *published in 1961. Mr. Long was born in Cambridge, Massachusetts, in 1910 and received his A.B. and Ph.D. degrees from Harvard University.*

of the United States in such a way that the diversity of environmental values will receive more effective representation in the decision-making structure of government.

The United States has become an overwhelmingly urban and preponderantly metropolitan nation, and will in all probability become overwhelmingly metropolitan. It is certainly clear that the institutions developed in Anglo-American constitutional history were not designed to deal with either the technology or the emergent culture of the modern United States.

Certain kinds of conflicts are built into the effort to maintain or improve the environment. Insofar as we think of the environment as physical, solutions usually are possible. But it is not enough to know the appropriate technical means; the area in which the methods are to be applied must be sufficiently comprehensive to permit a solution. Consequently, at the level of technical competence there is need for different areal solutions. This raises a whole string of questions about the propriety of governments being multipurpose affairs. Furthermore, it is very difficult to satisfy all the lines of preference, let alone optimize on them, because the preferences themselves are in conflict. We do not have any clear-cut common set of values.

Americans are only now in the business of building such values. Today these values have much more potentiality for being given political recognition than they have had previously. The Vietnamese war and possibilities of further escalation apart, our society can afford considerable expenditures to achieve kinds of qualities we desire if we can become sufficiently united in desiring certain kinds of end products of public goods. The problem is one of how to develop a sufficient amount of public support at the right level that has the resource capability, the political power, and the legal jurisdiction to take the kind of actions that the technical people say are required for accomplishing these purposes.

I rather suspect that the answer is largely a matter of leadership— of providing some kinds of new standards for people who up to the present had thought they were doing pretty well. Disagreement among the experts may be one of the major problems that the politicians have to face. A country that has so little concern about the environment of its lungs in the face of the statistics produced by the Surgeon General is likely to be less impressed, I think, with the question of the environment outside its lungs.

If we could move to a Brave New World in which we could simply say, "We trust our experts; they know;" we should not wait for scientific evidence. If we had even scientific fears, that would be enough: We would act immediately, even if the consequences affected life a hundred years ahead. But if we should do all this we would be very gravely changing the quality of the American political life.

That kind of asserted claim for the authority of the experts goes beyond any scientific warrant in terms of public verifiability or of the way in which conclusions can be arrived at. I think concern with this is one of the reasons why many of those who haven't been trained to middle class acquiescence in expertise voted in a hostile fashion in the fluoridation referenda that Gilbert White mentions in his essay.

We are moving into a society whose politics is going to be characterized by half-educated members of the middle class who have been able to afford to go to some kind of college. We can expect that as a result there will be a considerable increase in demand for expertise, and in docility before expertise.

Nonetheless, we must not let this carry us to the point where the voting public ceases to be deeply concerned with measures for checking on the experts and verifying their conclusions on what should be controlled and what should not be controlled, instead of just assuming that the doctor knows best, rather than the patient. As citizens we are patients, and while in every case the expert may know a great deal more than the patient about some one subject, every expert is himself a patient outside of his expertise. Our society is made up of the nonexperts in area after area, and these areas will grow as expertise grows. One of the deepest of current problems is that of how to maintain a democratic society in a world of experts in which the democratic society can be reasonably convinced that it is being persuaded rather than manipulated, and in which the institutions that generate, criticize, and control the expertise are adequate. Only then can society repose some kind of faith that the scientific processes that are being carried on are adequate and credible, and the intellectual processes by which people make decisions are not those of achieving consensus through crisis, through fear and through manipulation.

We have as a society been manipulated and we are being manipulated; this is being done by people who, with the best of intentions and in a great hurry, are concerned about the way in which they can save us from our folly.

Our traditional structure of government is to a very considerable extent designed to maximize vetoes, to maximize our capacity for saying "No," for disrupting, for preventing things from happening. This has its uses, but from the point of view of accomplishing things, and doing urgently needed things, it is a very serious liability. Changes are in order, and there are signs that a beginning is being made.

A major federal function is the activation of local publics whose existence makes possible the realistic political enterprise of pressing for needed public goods that have been underevaluated or not valued at all. The density and communication nets of elite populations at the Washington-New York political and media level make it possible to exert style leadership that is usually only feasible under the gun of dire necessity elsewhere. Rachel Carson's *Silent Spring,* like Upton Sinclair's *The Jungle,* could have far greater impact on the elite national media and the relevant Washington elites than it would have in most state capitals. A major policy initiative for Washington is the determination of what is the case, the dissemination in intelligible form of the facts and what they mean, and the development of standards as to minimal goals and further ranges of desirability. As Franklin Roosevelt once said, the Presidency is the best pulpit in the land and the message on environmental quality can nowhere be given more effective attention.

The job is one of giving saliency to neglected but potentially popular political issues and thus making it possible and even necessary for state and local politicians to take up the task of moving the issues at the local level. National politicians, elected and bureaucratic, at any rate some of them, have constituencies—both local and those reached through the media—that make various aspects of environmental quality feasible and attractive public goods for them to promote.

Their constituencies may often conflict, as would be the case with the automotive industry and its governmental allies and those seeking to enforce expensive devices to lessen exhaust fumes. The range of forces lined up pro and con on the issue of pesticides is illustrative of the internal conflict that differing bureaucratic constituencies produce within the federal establishment. But the fact that manufacturers and farmers fail to stifle inconvenient protests underlines the peculiar value of Washington as a center for wide and varied representation of positions that only achieve strength and visibility in a national theater.

There is some evidence that the President is aware of the highly limited range of the indicators that are at present included in his reports to the Congress and the public. The statistics are narrowly economic and even narrow within economics. A State of the Union message that deals with a more inclusive and more broadly relevant body of data representing the human condition is badly needed. The philistinism that has concerned itself more with statistical accuracy than relevance, and that has eschewed the qualitatively significant for the quantitatively measurable, distorts the public definitions of the situations that confront us. We are in important ways the prisoners of the measures that now determine the facts we collect and hence the limited and peculiar range of facts to which we attend.

Indicators of environmental quality need to be built into the national public reporting system at the Presidential level. This would be a major policy and institutional change, for it would place front and center a definition of what the situation is and what it is becoming. The fact that measurements cannot be precisely made is no excuse for not making them, especially if what is possible is vastly better than doing nothing. We need to realize that standards are tools that serve our purposes and are created out of human efforts. They do not emerge fully accredited from nature. To await such a miracle is to avoid the necessary political task of hammering out agreement on purposes and the necessarily imperfect, but improvable, means of their attainment.

As the disposer of the greatest pool of relatively painlessly collected tax surplus in the country, the federal government has the greatest freedom from fiscal constraint in its initiatives. As the jurisdiction that includes all others, the federal government internalizes the costs of the ills of environmental quality and the benefits from their removal. The United States can meaningfully calculate the costs of man days lost through illness or strikes and the gain in national product from the reduction of these limitations on the economy's performance. Similarly, the costs of air pollution and the inefficiencies of waste disposal are at least roughly calculable and the benefits, including increased federal fiscal resources from the reduction of this illth, are subject to determination sufficiently persuasive to suffice for rational policy making. We have long since realized that repetitive flood hazards are worth dealing with even though federal rather than local funds carry the lion's share of the burden.

A Milton Friedman type of analysis might suggest that the particularized investment of the nation's capital in a particular area amounts to an unsound interference with free market determination of location. There is merit in the concern that federal policy with respect to environmental quality may become another rivers and harbors or urban renewal program in which the logic of political expediency becomes the paramount logic. A contest for limited prizes can be the reality that masquerades under the cloak of general national policy. The political arithmetic of the situation could result in the illusion of a national policy and the reality of an expedient division of the loaves and the fishes. Yet the stimulation of the public appetite may be the first prerequisite to sufficient public support for adequate funding to pursue a truly national policy. Alternatively the winners of the contest for federal prizes may produce demonstrations that will inspire other local governments to emulate them even at their own expense.

Ambiguities as to which of these two policies are intended by federal politicians are rife in many national programs. The Poverty Program with its initial 90 per cent and subsequently diminishing federal share is a good example. No one knows for sure whether the federal phase-out is a gambit to pass the legislation through Congress that will be removed if public demand develops in the way hoped for, or whether it is just bait to get local governments to increase and enter into new programs that they will then have to fund from their own resources.

At one level the ambiguities in policy can be regarded as part of the national process of search by which individual and institutional actors respond to challenges and opportunities in the environment. Just as the mixed bag of contradictory policies thrown up by the New Deal seemed to offend against rational planning so today's mixed bag is likely to look like so much expedient politics as the actors involved in air and water pollution, pesticides, urban transport, blight, and aesthetics maneuver for advantage in terms of their various perspectives. The politically expedient is a mainspring of the technology through which we get things done. The number of tries is related to the likelihood that one of them will work and catch on if our social editing devices destroy the monsters and the drones that are bound to be produced. The Darwinism of social adjustment to change looks crude and untidy, but we lack alternatives.

Given the ambiguity of policy, those with a purpose in mind must press for its clarification. The federal policies in agriculture, rivers and harbors, and urban renewal are so many examples of a manifest policy that merely covers the satisfaction of latent pressure group ends. Whether broad general publics concerned with manifest goals can overcome their distortion by latent pressure group interests is always problematic. The likely payoff is in terms of symbolic recognition of broad goals with material representation of narrower purposes entertained by those capable of mobilizing sustained influence at critical places. Representation of environmental quality goals requires their institutionalization in the committees of Congress, the bureaucracy and the routines of the President.

From the point of view of the federal bureaucracy, the various aspects of environmental quality are so many items of new or expanded business. These items represent opportunities for some, threats for others. Minimally, as additional charges on the budget, they contend for scarce resources with other end items as diverse as the moon race and the war in Vietnam. In addition, they throw the apple of discord into the bureaucracy as departments and bureaus contend for jurisdiction. The departments and their bureaus are deeply set in institutionalized habits of thought and procedure. In addition, their allies, both among pressure groups and the organs of state and local governments, insure differential representation of interests, values and points of view. It was for reasons such as these that the friends of urban transportation legislation fought long and hard to keep their enterprise from the Department of Commerce and its committees on the Hill. The fragmentation of the aspects of environmental quality control among the federal departments presents ultimate problems of program co-ordination among institutions who not only compete among themselves, but are frequently committed to buttressing the status quo of their local friends. Appraisal of the alternatives for the institutionalization of the various aspects of environmental quality control in Washington requires a shrewd appreciation of the facts of bureaucratic life.

The contenders for a share in the emerging political market for environmental quality control are first and foremost the departments of Housing and Urban Development; Health, Education, and Welfare; Commerce; Interior; Agriculture; and Labor, with the rest such as NASA and the Department of Defense competitors for funds and objects for co-ordination rather than principals. However, even here, recognition should be given to DOD's role in sparking the Poverty Program, and its interest in alternative markets for its suppliers in the event of military cutbacks. In the short run, DOD and NASA are likely to appear in an adversary role in their claims against the budget for Vietnam and space. The hearings before the Reuss committee indicate that the Administration is not likely to support a shift in research and development expenditures toward the solution of environmental problems. Some testimony went to show that further research made little sense until present knowledge had been utilized. Whether the attitude toward R & D expenditures would extend to federal funding to secure greater use of existing knowledge is logically a separate question. However, given Vietnam a negative response seems likely. Of course Vietnam and a major Asian war overhang not just environmental quality control programs but the Great Society and society itself. Down the road, funds freed from DOD and possibly NASA will be available as well as other funds from growth in federal tax income.

Among the federal competitors for the job of environmental quality control, the Housing and Urban Development Department seems the most likely candidate for the job of administration and co-ordination. Health, Education, and Welfare, as the federal government's health department and the locus of the Public Health Service, will certainly have a technical research and in all probability some administrative concern with the health aspects of air and water pollution. Commerce's failure to capture urban transportation was a victory for the central cities and a blow to the Bureau of Public Roads and its allies. The conflict between central cities and suburbs is embedded in the constituencies of the two agencies. Suburbs, state governments, and the Bureau of Public Roads have long worked together. The effects of the "one man—one vote" doctrine will increase suburban power in state legislatures and decrease that of central cities.

The importance of the conflict between central cities and suburbs is not limited to probable acute differences over desirable transportation policy. Choice of emphasis on rail and mass transit will have major consequences for air pollution as well as transport. Beyond this, and even more important, the central city forces are likely to support regional approaches to transport planning. The success of mass transit depends on such an approach. As Lyle Fitch and his associates have pointed out, effective transport planning implies land use control. Such control is also highly desirable for any effective waste disposal or air pollution control program. There are joint political costs involved and there may well need to be a critical governmental press for an effective co-ordinated attack to be possible.

The constituency of the Housing and Urban Development Department is likely to be the 212 metropolitan areas where the bulk of our population already live and will increasingly live. This constituency is also the constituency of the President and it forms a vital element in the constituency of most senators. At present these 212 metropolitan areas are more census statistics than political entities. They are, however, potential communities. They share common problems whose effective solution may require common action of an area-wide nature. Of course there is no certainty that shared problems will produce a co-operation rather than adversary and divisive action. There are powerful reasons limiting cooperation to piecemeal and ad hoc palliatives.

Most federal programs have been directed at urban areas, and one might even say most federal programs have been piecemeal, ad hoc, and by way of exceptional interventions. These actions have been taken through the spending power with some constitutional bad conscience. While marble-cake federalism is currently gaining a measure of acceptance, the normal view was one of fairly clear-cut separation of levels and appropriate competences of government. Federal intervention still raises hackles. The ideology of sovereign states with their local governments was compounded by the general lip service to the politico-economic ideology of laissez faire. A truly national government has emerged from a federation of states without a theory to replace the outworn ideology, and this national government is groping towards the creation of a *national* system of local government compounded of the inherited political institutions, the pattern of state and local government. Much of what has been done in the past has served to buttress the institutional status quo by fiscally bailing it out and making it viable. There are now signs of impatience with this result and awareness of the need and possibility to exert creative pressure for the restructuring of our local institutions and the creation of a national system of local government responsive to the range of demands that are nationally salient but require local implementation.

A major force working against restructuring local governments into regional patterns whose resources and territories would be more adequate to achieve control of the quality of the physical environment is the deep-rooted desire to maintain inequalities in the human environment. Our society is committed to the two conflicting norms of equality and achievement. The commitment to equality has meant formal and increasingly substantive equality among citizens. The commitment to achievement has meant inequality among incomes. The latter in the past has been given effect mainly through the market by the device of rationing through price. With the increasing significance of public goods, e.g. schools, the problem has been how to give effect to unequal incomes in their consumption. The equality norm among citizens has presented increasing obstacles to providing a differential range of public goods to differing income holders in the same jurisdiction. While in the past and to a considerable degree today, public goods are not equalized to all citizens in the same jurisdiction, the pressure and the burdens mount. The answer to the problem has been found in the territorial segregation of public goods consumption—in a word, suburbs.

Those who would like control of the physical quality of the environment, air and water pollution, and even transport, are fearful of the further political consequences of creating institutions of the power and comprehensiveness requisite to the job. Metropolitan Toronto was a spectacular success as long as its George Washington Gardener was able to keep to sewerage, water and transport. A metropolitan public works department headed by a Bob Moses with a staff like that of the Port of New York Authority is a viable middle class ideal. But now that Toronto is moving from concrete to redistribution, the success story is running into difficulties. As things are, housing determines education, education determines jobs and marriage, jobs and marriage determine income, and income determines housing. As a number of political scientists and sociologists have begun to point out, the metropolitan area is an admirable array of governments with differential services to fit the pocketbook of our range of incomes. One buys one's house or rents one's apartment and the government goes with it, like membership in the country club. Most important, a quality school goes with a quality neighborhood, and the differential exposure of one's children to those one feels will do them the most good in work, socializing, and matrimony. This is a highly desired quality of an environment.

It is only to be expected that those for whom the quality of the environment that counts is access to housing, schools, jobs, income, and upward mobility should wish to use governmental change as a means to promote a breakthrough into the charmed circle. Those, on the other hand, who benefit from their position in the charmed circle by differential access to the opportunity structure, are highly reluctant to countenance its change. Suburbs are frequently willing to avail themselves of city water and sewerage, but resist bitterly central city attempts to use these assets as leverage to bring about annexation or a redistribution of public burdens. Suburbs are also fearful of extension of mass transit, because lowered cost of transport might produce a change in their population mix. On the other hand, central city Negroes with increasing political power are less and less willing to risk this increase of power through dilution in a white metropolitan area.

Given the suburban goals, it is readily understandable that piecemeal ad hoc solutions, single purpose districts, authorities, and unifunctional governmental departments make sense. The existing pattern of federal intervention has followed this line. Areal impacts of Washington programs have been co-ordinated neither nationally nor in the field. The Bureau of Public Roads and the Housing Agency have frequently worked at cross purposes. They and their allies in the states and local government have shown remarkably little interest in regional planning. Some lip service is now being given to the desirability of meshing programs to produce long-term foreseeable regional results. In the past, and to a large extent still, programs have been used to provide federal aid for favored participants in the battle to preserve and enhance positions in the local status quo. Thus urban renewal has frequently been used by hard pressed central city mayors to bulldoze out segments of their "tax eating" poor and replace them with the inhabitants of low service, high tax yield, luxury apartments. Even highway programs have been used as a kind of ruthless form of slum clearance.

A further problem for the improvement of environmental quality beyond the conflict over the politics of redistribution stems from the capabilities and motivations of local governments and their inhabitants. In our highly and increasingly mobile society, the marginal commitment of many residents makes long-term investment in major public goods a dubious proposition. As on the old frontier, the modern frontiersman of suburbia finds the solution to his problems in wearing the shine off his FHA or VA insured mortgaged tract house and escaping the consequences of the septic tank culture by moving on. Public officials responding to such constituencies are rarely in a position to live for more than from hand to mouth even when they are technically competent to entertain more professional standards of civic housekeeping. Again the resources of suburbia have not even a close fit with governmental needs.

The marginal middle class, the upper working class mortgaged to the hilt for housing and consumer capital goods, has more than enough to handle in meeting the sharply mounting school costs its child-centered culture entails. The cycle of septic tanks, piecemeal low cost inadequate solutions, and eventual areal solutions with cumulatively mounting costs is typical. Experience in the Seattle metropolitan area and in that of Minneapolis–St. Paul indicates that even highly educated suburbs heavily discount the future. Of course, it is standard to show little concern for the sewerage that pollutes one's neighbors' beaches and water supply. Detroit and the state of Michigan hold Chicago to account before the Supreme Court for diverting waters of Lake Michigan to dilute and divert its sewage while merrily polluting Lake Erie themselves.

Local governments are afflicted with what Edward Banfield termed the moral basis of a backward society immoral familism. In plain English this means every man for himself and the devil take the hindermost. If all could be trusted to co-operate, all might benefit and the game would be transformed from zero sum to multiple payoff. However, when the edifice of trust is hopelessly shaky or nonexistent, Machiavelli is the better guide. Indeed, a regional plan which locates the industrial park in one town and the open space in another, and fails to provide for the pooling of tax yield is an exercise in utopian futility. The existing structure of local government is territorially and fiscally inadequate to undertake in any major way to improve the quality of the environment. The very well meaning conferences and the useful informal relations among the professionals of local government can do little more than help the status quo to rock along.

Beyond the adequacy of territorial and fiscal resources, local governments are limited by the availability of elite populations, institutions and media to sustain the kinds of concern involved in improving the quality of environments in other than response to crisis and on piecemeal and ad hoc bases. The problems to which governments attend are as James G. Coke has shown likely to be phenomena of scale. Coke (in *The Lesser Metropolitan Areas of Illinois,* University of Illinois Institute of Government and Public Affairs, 1962) found that the smaller cities of Illinois were suffering from all the problems of core decay, grey areas and suburban sprawl that afflicted the large metropolis. However, the problems of these smaller cities failed to achieve articulation by reason of lack of density of relevant elite population of architects, planners and groups likely to form citizens' housing councils and like organizations. Local government fragmentation can have the effect of so dispersing elite populations and limiting media effect in concentrating issues that concern with the improvement of environment quality is politically realistic only at the level of the national government and some central cities.

The realistic promotion of improvement in the quality of environment is most likely to achieve its lead from Washington. The Housing and Urban Development Department promises to become the American equivalent of a ministry of local government. The federal carrot and stick can be used to promote the reality of planning at the metropolitan level and, where technically required by the problem, in jurisdictions that include relevant watersheds or drainage basins.

Improving the quality of the environment in the 212 metropolitan areas where most of the people of the United States live is a realistic objective for the new agency. If, as is projected, it regionalizes to these areas and staffs its regional executives at the assistant secretary level, it has an excellent chance of becoming the chosen arm for presidential field co-ordination. Should the President use the Department in this way, the President would for the first time have an instrument for effectuating the field co-ordination and the Washington co-ordination of the impact of the disparate federal programs on our cities.

The tools available range from personnel to funds for planning, housing, public facilities, highways, and research. Federal funds in the past have not been used to promote governmental integration at the local level. Constitutional scruples may still cause some to shy away from a deliberately concerted federal effort to restructure local government so as to make it more effective in promoting improvement in the quality of the environment. Doubtless, there will be considerable circumlocution in the public relations presentation of the objective. Some such device as the "workable program" concept developed in urban renewal (though the latter has tended to be a sham) could be adapted to planning and effectuating regional sewerage and water programs, transportation, air pollution, housing, open space, and such other federally assisted local programs as need regional planning effectively carried into action to amount to anything. Since most of the programs required for improving the quality of the environment would benefit greatly from it if they do not demand land use control, there is a powerful argument for placing overall planning and responsibility in a single agency. It is possible that the fears of a local politics of redistribution and the ingrained habits of rugged individualism may not prove insuperable.

The restructuring of local government to provide jurisdictions with the territory, the fiscal ability, and the motivation to improve the quality of the environment will move ahead more rapidly if it avoids commitment to any doctrinaire, uniform panacea. In many cases the states may prove the most promising level of government for achieving metropolitan integration. This is likely to be the case in Massachusetts where some 60 per cent of the state's population is included within the Boston metropolitan area. It is certainly the case with Rhode Island. While the "one man—one vote" doctrine is likely to strengthen the suburbs as against the central cities, it is not inevitable that the states will continue unresponsive to the needs of a politics of redistribution. Clearly, for water resource development, quite probably for efficient drainage basin management, and probably for reserving and developing open space, there must be a major role for the states if for no other reason because of their legal powers and the likely need to use interstate compacts in many cases.

Perhaps more important than the likely suburban bias of state legislatures is the orientation and prestige of the old-line agencies and bureaucrats in the states and even in the local governments. These normally worship at the shrines of the gods of things as they are. Much can be done by the federal government to change program emphasis by using the carrot of funds along with provisions for personnel that insure professional competence and appropriate compensation. Much can be done from Washington to induce upgrading of environmental improvement functions at city, county, and state levels through grants with controls. The achievement of some modicum of institutionalized professional elite at state and local levels is a prerequisite to the activation and direction of potential publics and the instruction and programming of the media. Much of the professionalism that exists in many states owes its existence to federal grants with merit requirement strings.

Representation of the emerging functions of environmental control at appropriate levels in state and local bureaucracies is essential to counterbalancing entrenched representatives of habitual methods of handling highway and other activities with little or no regard for the newly emerging concerns. It is probably wiser to attempt to create allies in the state bureaucracies than to attempt to completely bypass them. Experience with the Poverty Program indicates that the bypass route may prove ultimately more costly than the longer road of developing compatible counterpart units in the states.

Placing of research funds with state and other universities and private industry at least potentially increases knowledge and lowers the costs of attaining goals. It also broadens the base of those with an informed concern about environmental quality. Activated elites in academic and university circles are especially effective in the dissemination of ideas. Since much of the problem of obtaining improvement depends on the creation of elite and general public opinion favoring such an enterprise, funds directing the interest of strategically placed elites toward the problems are likely to bear fruit all out of proportion to their amount. An informed concern with environmental quality is badly needed in industry because in many cases the most serious and uncontrollable offenders are in the private sector.

Many local and even state governments are reluctant to tackle the problems of industrial pollution for fear of reducing their attractiveness as a location for industry. Indeed, many industries have capitalized their permission to inflict their wastes on others, as many slum properties have capitalized their failure to meet codes. In both cases any sudden crack-down could produce painful and even disastrous increases in costs. Beyond this, if competing locations can offer freedom from desirable standards, many communities will put jobs and tax revenues ahead of pollution abatement. It may well be that only the federal government can provide the sanctions that will free state and local governments from paralyzing fear of economic loss.

There seems little doubt that the costs of controlling waste disposal whether into the air, into water, or so-called nondegradable objects like tin cans will be steeply increasing in the affluent society. If the cost could be internalized to industry, the problem of policing by government could be enormously simplified. The insurance companies and their counterpart units in industry are probably far more effective in achieving plant safety than is state inspection. When pollution control becomes a routinely calculable cost of industry, represented in the corporate decision-making hierarchy rather than a governmental threat to be parried by house counsel and public relations, progress will be expedited. This would suggest federal tax incentives, either in the form of write-off or credit to induce investment or of nuisance taxation to penalize pollution. The receipts of the latter tax could be returned to states or local governments with appropriate legislation and administration.

It is likely that industry's own ranks will be increasingly divided over pollution. At least the growing tourist industry is likely to be more and more concerned with environmental quality. States that used to show a tender regard for the convenience of pulp mills and power companies are waking up to the competing lucrative uses of their streams. There are few more rabid groups than fishermen who, in their frenzy, even assault reservoirs for drinking water. The affluent society is producing a mass leisure public with a capacity for appreciation of environmental quality. To be sure, the affluence of this society produces the rocketing energy consumption and waste production that it is now affluent enough to find objectionable. Doubtless, this could result in a stand-off. Conceivably the cost of waste disposal could approach the cost of energy consumed. One can only hope that the affluent society's waste will not bring about its cumulative impoverishment. Estimates of hot waste disposal from atomic power (whose increase could be fantastic) are so high that little careful thought seems to be now given to it.

As the U.S. Department of Agriculture runs out of farmers it seems, like other organizations, to search for new customers to keep it going. The same holds true for the land-grant universities and colleges. Recent regional conferences held under the auspices of land-grant institutions have brought together people from the departments of Agriculture and Interior and the Corps of Engineers to consider the problems and possibilities of planning for people in nonmetropolitan areas. Fifty million or more Americans live outside the standard metropolitan areas. These too are a constituency for environmental improvement. Karl Fox at Iowa State has pressed for the significant possibilities of planning in these nonmetropolitan areas. There seems to be a significant responsibility that might be met by the Department of Agriculture and some other departments in acting as the Washington sponsors for this area of local government. Existing relations with state government make likely a favorable climate for cooperation. The concern of many of these areas with tourism gives promise of influence on the state legislatures that will favor some aspects of environmental quality improvement.

The improvement of the quality of the environment is a high priority goal in giving reality to the conception of a Great Society. The articulation of this goal and its gradual development through standards and reporting is a necessity for developing the state of public opinion. The new Department of Housing and Urban Development can be expected to make this issue a major objective of important programs. The opinion leadership of Washington and its fiscal assistance can only go part way. The development of metropolitan or regional governments that can afford, and be motivated to undertake, the improvement of the quality of environment is the major institutional requisite for serious and fundamental action.

Jacob H. Beuscher

SOME NEW MACHINERY TO HELP DO THE JOB

Professor Long is a cautious pilot. He sees and respects the shoals, and rocks, and cross currents of American political life. He has sensible regard for the vital importance in political affairs of a constituency if policy and institutional changes are to be accomplished. The confusing pluralism that results from inter-bureau competition; the rivers and harbors hand-out approach; the rationing of federal grants-in-aid on the basis not of need but of political geography; the inevitability of wasteful, pluralistic, overlapping measures—all of these facts of American political life he recognizes.

But in spite of these and other navigational hazards, Professor Long has an affirmative general course to propose as we fumble toward the goals of improved environmental quality.

He places principal reliance upon the federal government. It is at this level that problems are to be identified, research conducted, standards determined, and information disseminated. An especially important function is assigned to the Presidential pulpit, and the need for new standards and ways of measuring is especially acute if this pulpit is to be made as effective as it can be.

Jacob H. Beuscher, *professor of law at the University of Wisconsin, has been a member of the law faculty there since 1935. He specializes in property law and the relation of law to the allocation and use of natural resources. From 1958 to 1962 he directed a detailed study of water rights in Minnesota, Wisconsin, Ohio, and Indiana, and currently is active in a University interdepartmental seminar on river basin planning. Through the Wisconsin Legislative Council and the State Department of Resource Development he has worked with state and university experts on numerous reports and bills concerned with land and water. He has written two books on law as it relates to agriculture, and is editor of a set of materials on land use controls. Mr. Beuscher was born in Cudahy, Wisconsin, in 1907. He received his A.B. and LL.B. degrees from the University of Wisconsin and his S.J.B. from Yale University.*

Only the federal government has the fiscal freedom and the comprehensive reporting service to demonstrate the ills of environmental quality and the benefits of their removal. Here alone is it possible to mobilize sustained influence through committees of Congress, the bureaucracy and the routines of the President. Only at the federal level is it possible successfully to adjust between the norm of *equality* that typically characterizes the "have nots" and the norm of achievement which characterizes those who have a deep-rooted desire to maintain inequalities in the human environment. In spite of bureaucratic competition, and geographical imbalance, the possibility exists that the vast spending power of the Congress can be used (1) to exert creative pressure for the evolution of a "national system of local government" and (2) to set up demonstration programs for state and local guidance.

I have these general comments:

First, Professor Long's warnings based on keen political insight are more specific than his affirmative suggestions for institutional innovation. I shall bumble into the brambles which the wise man avoids.

Second, I think we can easily agree that new and "ideal" institutional arrangements do not automatically bring about an improved or protected environment. Success can be assured only by qualified, aggressive, and enthusiastic personnel who are dedicated to program objectives.

Finally, I agree completely that the dominant role must be that of the federal government, but I would assign to the states important secondary roles. Many states have been relatively dormant in the field of environmental quality, but not all. Our intensive studies of the day-to-day administration of Wisconsin's water pollution laws, for example, demonstrate a considerable degree of accomplishment. The dormant states must be prodded and bribed into action by the federal government. This as a matter of fact is happening in water pollution, land and water conservation, state planning and other programs. The states are important in at least the following respects:

As important repositories of "residual sovereignty," the states share constitutional powers needed as supplement to federal power, particularly in the land use field. They are the chief custodians of the common law of property and of contract, the constant reshaping and remolding of which is vital to environmental quality programs.

States, as distinguished from amorphous metropolitan areas, are important rallying points for subconstituencies. The states have the capacity to take the place of, and play the roles of, metropolitan regional government—a type of government which thirty years of talk has failed to bring into existence. If after all this the dream of regional government is still to be realized, the states will have to make it a reality. The states, better than the metropolitan regions (though not as effectively as the federal government) can tackle tough conflicts between those relegated to dirty neighborhoods and those battling to protect their nice, clean, well scrubbed, upper middle class suburbs.

Most environmental quality problems must be approached in terms of the specific variables and data and analysis and characteristics of the particular locale, the so-called problem shed. Often the technical data and know-how needed to wrestle with the local scientific, engineering, economic, ethnic, and legal specifics are available only in the state capital.

If we are to have problem-shed organizations larger than a city or a county, the states must be relied on to create them whether for intra-state or interstate problem sheds. Interstate compacts require state consent and state support, intra-state organizations require enabling legislation. (One must recognize, however, that interstate regional organizations may require years to evolve sufficient constituency to support an effective action program.)

The federal government already operates several direct regulatory programs affecting the quality of the environment. Air and water pollution control are illustrations. Less direct is federal "regulation" of land uses through FHA building codes and neighborhood standards and urban renewal contracts. These regulatory efforts are in addition to its vast grant-in-aid, and major data-gathering and research contributions. Probably in the foreseeable future the federal government will expand these programs and conceivably undertake additional direct regulatory programs. For example, failure of the states to do an adequate job of flood plain regulation may spawn a federal program of flood plain insurance and regulation applicable at least to lands along navigable waters of the United States. As such direct regulatory activity expands we can expect some experimentation with joint federal-state regulatory mechanisms. The joint board for the determination of stream pollution standards under the Water Quality Act of 1965 may be a forerunner of such joint mechanisms. Drawing on joint-board experience in the motor carrier regulatory field, we may see created, particularly for major interstate problem-shed areas, state-federal investigatory and adjudicative teams and boards, for water and air pollution abatement, for the regulation of pesticides and other thinly spread pollutants, and for solid-waste disposal and management.

We also need within the Office of the President a Council of Environmental Advisers. As Professor Long indicates, the Office of the President is a logical center for a co-ordinated national reporting system on environmental quality. In the absence of such a co-ordinating mechanism, there will be separate caches of pertinent scientific, engineering economic, and other data in a number of agencies. Besides, as Professor Long also points out, standards and indicators of danger need to be evolved. As he says, they will not emerge fully accredited from nature. Where the environmental problem involves more than one bureau, as it often does, we cannot rely on separate agencies to cross bureaucratic lines. As technology constantly changes, we need to bring together related facts and set integrated standards. When line responsibilities are assigned to public agencies in the resource or environmental field the agencies become myopic to problems. They also are prone rather quickly to fill up the assigned regulatory field with lots of rules and regulations, and then to be rather unresponsive to change indicated by new technological knowledge.

So it would be well to have in the Office of the President a small group of highly trained scientists, economists, and public administration experts as technical integrators constantly checking with the data collectors, the analyzers, the certifiers, the standard makers and the regulators in the various federal agencies. They would keep a centralized bank of selected data, check out interrelationships that might escape the individual agencies and report to the President, thus making his pulpit more effective. They would also recommend to the President, as needed, the appointment of special task forces for particular environmental evaluations.

Also needed at the national level, but outside government, is a foundation-financed Environmental Action Clearing House. Its library on environmental quality would be complete and current. Its reports would present in laymen's oversimplified terms central issues and problems in the field. It would be a source of up-to-date information about institutional experimentation and innovation in the field, including new administrative and legal techniques. For example, the latest information on open space easements, effluent charges, flood plain regulation, and scenic zoning would be available here.

If the states are to play a more vital role in the field of environmental quality, there must not only be a flow of federal money downward to them, but also a reassembled flow of power back upward from local to state government. Allocation of power between states and their local units is not static. It is in constant flux. (This phenomenon deserves more scholarly attention than it gets.)

States have almost completely abdicated zoning and subdivision control powers to local units. They have also left to local units, often weak, the tough task of dealing with shrewd and often powerful land developers.

Induced by federal grants-in-aid, there should be some reassembling of land use control and negotiating powers by the states. Already this is happening for bands of land along main highways, to protect against indiscriminate access and to carry out the purposes of the highway beautification program.

Also badly needed is direct state intervention and regulatory control over lands in watercourse corridors for the protection of shorelands, water quality, flood plains, and wetlands.

In this country we have operated on the assumption that it was enough to give to the states power to regulate municipal and industrial polluters of our streams. We have ignored the individual septic tank as a source of pollution of our lakes, and certainly we have ignored the "pollution" of the environment which occurs when private development destroys scenic and amenity values both in highway and in watercourse corridors. These omissions need to be rectified immediately. The states should assume and energetically carry out their roles of trustees over highway and watercourse corridor lands. To this end there need to be state level shoreland zoning and subdivision platting control, state level flood plain regulation, and state scenic, open space, and conservation easement purchase programs.

Direct state open space purchase programs are being greatly accelerated in a number of states. But something more is needed if we are to save open space areas in metropolitan regions for recreation, for amenities, for ground water recharge, and for other open space purposes. We need to put a single state agency in a position to negotiate and deal with those who propose to develop lands in designated critical areas. Such an agency needs a full packet of powers to regulate, to purchase fee or less than fee interests, to enter into tax arrangements and in general to work out planned unit development or other arrangements saving precious open space in the process.

In this connection what is happening in Massachusetts may be a wave of the future. Through two coastal waters laws and an inland water law, a major part of all of the land of the state has been subjected to state level approval before development can occur. In co-operation with state wildlife, fisheries, water quality, highway, and other technical personnel, hundreds of applications for development permission are being acted upon by the State Resource Commission. There is local review but ultimately it is the state which sits across the bargaining table from the developer.

Of course procedural and substantive rules of fair play should apply in such bargaining, and there should also be judicial review, but even within these rules, there is a real challenge to develop the bargaining technique at the state level, not only for water quality, air pollution and roadside corridors, but also for provision of open space and perhaps the solution of regional land problems that transcend local boundary lines.

If the states are really going to stay in the act—and I think they will stay in for a substantial period—they will have to match the federal government with an agency that can accommodate the specialized data needed to understand the interrelationships that I have mentioned earlier in connection with federal responsibilities. This at least is true of local data particularly pertinent to the problems within a state.

An increasing number of state planning agencies are being created largely because of Public Law 507-705, and some of them are completely staffed. These agencies might become the offices at the state level that deal with the Board of Environmental Advisers in the Office of the President.

Let me conclude, as would any good lawyer, by a reference to the possible role of the state courts in a program of environmental quality. As Ralph Turvey has pointed out, courts constantly shape and reshape the basic building blocks of our legal and economic institutions, of which property and contract seem to me to be the most important. In our system most of the shaping is done principally on a day-to-day basis by the state courts. And these courts have proven to us over and over again that property in this country is not just a basis for security of expectations and for maintenance of *status quo,* but is a concept that plays a dynamic role in a world of constant change.

Long before we set up administrative agencies to wrestle with water and air pollution or solid waste pollution, the courts were attempting, through a system of public and private rights, to protect people from at least the worse effects of the other fellow's residues. Without ever, so far as I know, using that pallid and abstract term "externalities," they have attempted to prevent the shifting onto innocent people at least the most obvious costs of pollution, costs which the courts see in terms of unhealthy, uncomfortable or unpleasant living, or perhaps of sharp interference with desired uses of land or other resources.

What more might the courts do in the field of pollution control? They obviously have serious limitations. They are not equipped with a technical staff. Only those cases which are brought to the court get decided, not those that somehow are settled first. The ownership boundaries of the land that is before the court demark each case and are apt to set the problem as the court sees it. The geographical limitations may be too constricted. The judge is not a technical man, and so forth. Nevertheless there is room for improvement.

The states, or at least some of them, might consider establishing on an experimental basis the much-discussed office of the Ombundsman, the public official who in Sweden receives and acts on private complaints, even to the extent of suing, at the Ombundsman's discretion, at the public expense. Also, the rules of legal procedure might be changed so that when a state standard has been set for water quality, air quality, or whatever, and where a private individual comes to court to contend that this standard is not being complied with, the burden of proof be on the polluter. It might also be worth providing that courts in such environmental quality nuisance cases be free to use existing administrative expertise at the state level. Courts might also be required to listen to, if it was offered, the testimony of economists on costs and benefits, though not bound to decide the case on the basis of this alone.

Legal standards administered by courts in pollution cases are very vague. The words "reasonable" and "substantial" hold sway, and the courts attempt to balance utility of conduct against gravity of harm. A prediction of what a court will do or will not do in a particular case under a particular set of locational, economic, social and aesthetic circumstances, is extremely risky. There should be some experiments with legislation that will attempt to establish these standards a bit more precisely and firmly. And in this connection it might be worth experimenting with an arrangement under which there would be only one court in the state to which pollution cases would come, and it might make sense for this court to be located in the state capital, where the state specialists and experts would be close by for the court to call on them as masters if it saw fit.

To sum up:

It is important to bring a great deal of the data about the quality of the enviroment into one place, to keep the information current and to establish some kind of an agency for continuous analysis of what this shows, particularly in terms of interrelationships.

Joint boards might be tried, at least as a forerunner of interstate compacts, as a device for carrying out direct regulatory programs that involve interstate areas.

We might experiment with the problem-shed approach. State governments might be used as substitutes for regional government in the handling of environmental problems in metroplitan regions that cannot be handled by any one unit in the region. And we might put the states in a position to bargain with private developers, at least for certain kinds of lands, and hope thereby to prevent in the future the kinds of environmental messes we have had in the past.

We might continue to experiment at the state level with co-ordinating mechanisms other than the joint board, so that federal and state agencies can effectively work together.

It is all right to keep the courts in the act, but don't expect too much from them.

NOTE: The recent publication of *Waste, Management and Control* by the National Academy of Sciences–National Research Council (Publ. 1400) has lightened my task. I refer the reader to Chapters 6 and 7 for additional suggestions for institutional innovation in the interest of environmental quality.

⟨ INDEX ⟩

for, ix; outputs from in the economic set, 6, 7, 10, 11
Crocker, Thomas D., 70n
Crowding: physiological and behavioral disturbances resulting from, 16, 27–29; adaptability to, 24
Czamanske, David, 110n, 113n

Damage of environment, viii, ix, xi; types of, 12–14, 16, 17; public concern over, 17; need of criteria for behavior toward, 18; need for control of, 24, 36; pathological consequences of, 25, 76–77; costs of, 73–76; effluent charges on, 89
Davidson, Paul, 75n
Davis, E. E., 124n
Davis, Robert K., 80n, 84n, 86
Defense: priority of in policy formulation involving the future, 12
Delaware River: as potable water source, 74; recreational value of, 75
Demsetz, Harold, 63
Detergents, 81–82
Developing countries: resource problems in, viii
Diets: man's capacity to adapt to malnutrition or overnutrition, 24, 26–27
Diseases: cancer and vascular diseases from air pollution, 25; pulmonary disease in industrialized areas, 25; from chemical pollution, 26; control of infectious diseases, 27; damage from microbial diseases, 27; advances in prevention and treatment of, 29; new diseases created by antimicrobial drugs, 30; changes in pattern and control of, 31
Dorfman, Robert, 77n, 100n
Douglas, William O., 134
Drug control, 35, 100
Dubos, René, xiii, 40, 41, 42
Duhl, Leonard J., xiii

Earth. See Planet Earth
Ecology of human society: changes in character of, 15–16; wholeness of, 40–41, 43; planning for, 43
Economic analysis of environmental quality: welcome and unwelcome results of economic growth, ix, xiii, 24; categories of studies, 69; importance of in decision-making, 75, 84, 86, 87

Economy of the human society: the "cowboy" economy characteristic of open societies, 9; the "spaceman" economy of the future, 9–10, 11, 12
Econosphere: processes involved in, 5, 6, 15
Elson, Ruth Miller, 113, 130n
Energy system: sources of inputs of, 4, 5–8; outputs of, 4, 5, 6; the Second Law of Thermodynamics in, 7
England: statement by Aviation Minister on noise tax on airports and soundproofing of private dwellings, 59–60; River Authorities in, 86; example of attitude toward public opinion, 133
Environmental-quality management: concept of optimality, 71, 73; costs of achieving ideals, 71; feasibility and equity, 72; information to the public by, 118, 124, 127; personality attributes ("affective complexity") as a factor in, 124, 127; decisions and actions by, 124–27; opinion-taking by, 133
Environmental stimuli: effects of on man's behavior, 121; exposure to as a limited activity, 136
Epidemiological surveys, 35, 36, 37
Erosion control, 121
Europe: diverse societies of as a base in acceleration of culture, 9
Externalities (spillovers) in resource use: internalizing the externality, 60, 63, 64; costs and gains, 63; control of, 64, 83, 90–91; government's handling of, 65
Exurbia: hazards of contaminated wells and septic tanks in, 95. See also Suburbia

Farm production: scale of as a threat to other human values, xii
Federal government in environmental field: intervention by, 20, 148, 150; actions of in resource use, 64–65; as influence on public action, 124; activation of local publics for needed public goods, 124, 144; fiscal resources of for reducing ills of environment, 145, 157; grants-in-aid provided by, 153, 156, 160; regulatory programs of, 158–59. See also United States